Alfred Mason Williams

Studies in Folk Song and Popular Poetry

Alfred Mason Williams

Studies in Folk Song and Popular Poetry

ISBN/EAN: 9783744772099

Printed in Europe, USA, Canada, Australia, Japan

Cover: Foto ©Thomas Meinert / pixelio.de

More available books at **www.hansebooks.com**

STUDIES IN FOLK-SONG AND POPULAR POETRY

BY

ALFRED M. WILLIAMS

AUTHOR OF "SAM HOUSTON AND THE WAR OF INDEPENDENCE IN TEXAS"

BOSTON AND NEW YORK
HOUGHTON, MIFFLIN AND COMPANY
The Riverside Press, Cambridge
1894

Copyright, 1894,
By ALFRED M. WILLIAMS.

All rights reserved.

The Riverside Press, Cambridge, Mass., U. S. A.
Electrotyped and Printed by H. O. Houghton and Company.

TO C. A. W.

*How oft have I in days forever gone
Heard thy pure voice in some old, simple song,
With happy sadness and sweet grief prolong
The dear complaint of some fond heart forlorn,
That wept in music from grief's harp-strings drawn;
While all the joys that to full bliss belong
Bloomed in thy radiant grace, a magic throng,
And love enwrapped thee in its shining morn.
But now, alas, those mournful strains of old
Touch my sad heart with pains it cannot bear;
Their music breathes the anguish they enfold,
And sorrow sings with each enchanted air,
While gleams the vision of that face so fair,
Those dear brown eyes, that hair of softened gold.*

NOTE.

Of the essays in this volume, that on American Sea Songs has been published in the Atlantic Monthly, and that on Folk-Songs of the Civil War in the American Folk-Lore Journal. Those on English and Scottish Popular Ballads, Lady Nairne and her Songs, and William Thom, the Weaver Poet, were contributed as literary articles to the Providence Sunday Journal. It may be thought that the essays on Sir Samuel Ferguson and Celtic Poetry, Lady Nairne, and William Thom do not come within the strict limits of folk-song and popular poetry, but they have a cognate interest as illustrating the development of folk-song in cultivated literature, and seem to me to be within a reasonable approximation to the title of the volume.

PROVIDENCE, R. I., *July* 12, 1894.

CONTENTS

	PAGE
AMERICAN SEA SONGS	1
FOLK-SONGS OF THE CIVIL WAR	36
ENGLISH AND SCOTTISH POPULAR BALLADS	71
LADY NAIRNE AND HER SONGS	102
SIR SAMUEL FERGUSON AND CELTIC POETRY	131
WILLIAM THOM, THE WEAVER POET	166
FOLK-SONGS OF LOWER BRITTANY	189
THE FOLK-SONGS OF POITOU	220
SOME ANCIENT PORTUGUESE BALLADS	242
HUNGARIAN FOLK-SONGS	282
FOLK-SONGS OF ROUMANIA	309

STUDIES IN FOLK-SONG AND POPULAR POETRY.

AMERICAN SEA SONGS.

Oh, fare ye well, my pretty, fair maids,
  I'm bound for the Rio Grande!
  Ri-o-Rio!
  I'm bound for the Rio Grande!

No one who is old enough to remember the glorious spectacle of a full-rigged American clipper ship getting under full sail outside of the headlands of a harbor, after having been cast off by the tug, is likely to have forgotten the sight: the white sails dropping from the yards, being sheeted home, and swelling out to the fresh wind, until a cloud of canvas sparkled in the sun; the strong and graceful life which the ship took on under their power; the foam curling up under the bow with her forward rush; the great plain of the ocean, with all its free airs and salt scents, beckoning to life and adventure seaward round the world. To this, to one on board or near enough to hear, will be added the indefinable and mysterious charm of the sailors' chants, as they haul in the bowline, and tauten up the tacks and sheets by a pull requiring unison of effort; and the cadence, at once long-drawn and vigorous, fills the air with a magic voice of the wind and the sea. It has the melopœism, if it may be so called, of the cadence of nature, and takes its note from the solitude and melancholy of the world, never more impressive than upon the vast plain of the sea. It has been heard from immemorial time, since the first oarsmen pulled together along the coasts of the Indian Ocean, and possesses the same essence in whatever language it is uttered; and, while it has its practical purpose in securing unison and accentuation of effort, it would be a mistake to suppose it without origin in and appeal to the innate impulse for the expression of sentiment in melody in the heart of man. Every sea captain knows, or used to know, how much more quickly the anchor came up, or how much more hearty were the pulls on the bowlines, if there were a full-lunged and melodious leader for the "shanty;" and his practical-minded mate would at times shout, when the chorus was going faintly and mechanically, "Sing out there, can't ye?" with the same purpose with which he would exhort the men to take a stronger pull. Conversely, a poor leader, or a second who could not or would not keep in proper time, was a decided injury to the effectiveness of the labor; and it sometimes happened that an energetic captain, when his ship was being got under way, would step up to a sailor, apparently heaving sturdily at the windlass, and knock him sprawling, for the reason that he had detected him giving the wrong time to the chant, out of mischief, or for the sake of testing the sharpness and intelligence of the "old man."

The words of these windlass and bowline "shanties" have, of course, little of the element of finished poetry about them. They are not songs, but chants, whose purpose is to give accentuation and force to the exertion of united strength rather than to the expression of sentiment, and of which the rhythmical melody is the essential element. Whether they be new or old, they always have been essentially improvisations, capable of being stopped at any moment or added to indefinitely, and, like the refrains of the old ballads, are dependent upon the sound rather than the sense for their effect. Nevertheless, however imperfect and indefinite their expression, they took their tone and color originally from the elements in which they were born, and gave out not only the voice of the sea and the wind, the notes of the never silent Æolian harp of the cordage and the bellying sails, but the prevailing sentiment of the human heart upon the great deep, its underlying oppression, its longing for home, its craving for relief from monotony; and it is a dull ear that would not detect this, under the most absurd and uncouth words ever strung together in a sailor's shanty.

As among the seamen of all races, the chants of the American sailors, before they were so reduced in quality and number by the combined influence of steam vessels and a protective tariff, were of ancient and indefinite origin, and were constantly being altered or added to by circumstance and improvisation. They came, of course, first from the English seamen, who were our sailors' ancestors and associates, to whom at least the element descended from the songs to which the galleys of the sea kings of Scandinavia were impelled over the foaming brine, or the Celtic coracle was paddled on the lonely lake; and it is impossible, in a mass of rude verse, of little definite meaning, of a fluid and fluctuating form, and handed down from lip to lip without ever, except incidentally, having been put into print and preserved, to fix the origin or the date of creation of any of these songs. There are traces of old phrases and archaisms, ancient words strangely metamorphosed into a semblance of modern meaning, and all such settlings and deposits as are to be found in the geological strata of spoken language, — references to mermaids, sea-serpents, and survival of myths regarding the powers of the sea and air; but they are of no such distinct historic value as are the indications to be found in the more definite folk-lore in prose or verse, which have the element of dramatic interest and narrative. It is to be remembered that these chants, as we have said, were essentially improvisations, with a purpose different from ordinary song,—that is, to give the governing power of melody to united exertion,—and that whatever color and substance they have are extraneous, and not inherent. What is distinctively American can be determined only by local allusions or by definite knowledge of their origin: the first are of very little value, for an English chant, with its local allusions, might be very readily altered into an American one by the substitution of American names; and in regard to the second, as has been said, the songs were born, and passed from mouth to mouth, and from ship to ship, without any one's knowing or caring where they originated. Nevertheless, the American sailors, when there were American sailors, had as strong a national and provincial feeling as those of any other country; were capable of making their own chants, if not as much given to improvisation as those of the Latin races; and had a selection of local names as sonorous and as readily adapted to the needs of a rhythmical chorus as those of any English-speaking people. The Rio Grande and the Shenandoah were as mouth-filling and sonorous as the High Barbaric or any of the refrains of the English shanties, and the American sailor sheeted home his canvas with Virginia Ashore, or Baltimore, or Down to Mobile Bay in his remembrance as well as on his lips.

Premising that American shanties are not American sea songs in any definite sense of the term, and fulfill only the conditions to which they are subject as aids to labor and stimulants to exertion, we may take a specimen or two to show what they were like. It is needless to say that neither the words nor a musical notation would give any idea of their effect when sung with full-throated chorus to sea and sky, and that their peculiar melodious cadence and inflection can be caught only by hearing them. Like the chants of the negro slaves, which they resemble in many respects, musical notes would give only the skeleton of the melody, which depends for its execution upon an element which it defies the powers of art to symbolize. They have various forms, — a continued and unbroken melody, as when turning the capstan or pumping, or they show an emphatic accentuation at regular intervals, as when stretching out a bowline with renewed pulls; and such as they are, they are given precisely as sung, with a dependence upon the reader's imagination to supply in some degree the cadence and accentuation. The following are good specimens of the bowline chants.

> *Solo.* I wish I was in Mobile Bay,
> *Chorus. Way*-hay, knock a man down!
> *Solo.* A-rolling cotton night and day,
> *Chorus. This* is the time to knock a man down!

And so on *ad infinitum,* until the hoarse " Belay! " of the mate or the " bosun " ends it.

> Oh, Shenandoah's a rolling river,
>   *Hooray,* you rolling river,
> Oh, Shenandoah's a rolling river,
>   *Ah-hah,* I'm bound away to the wild Missouri!
> Oh, Shenandoah's a packet sailor, etc.

> My Tommy's gone, and I'll go too,
>   Hurrah, you high-low!
> For without Tommy I can't do,
>   My Tommy's gone a high-low!
> My Tommy's gone to the Eastern shore,
>   *Chorus.*
> My Tommy's gone to Baltimore, etc.

A favorite and familiar pulling song is Whiskey for my Johnny: —

> Whiskey is the life of man,
>   *Whiskey-*Johnny!
> We'll drink our whiskey while we can,
>   *Whiskey* for my Johnny!
> I drink whiskey, and my wife drinks gin,
>   *Chorus.*

The way she drinks it is a sin,
Chorus.
I and my wife cannot agree,
Chorus.
For she drinks whiskey in her tea,
Chorus.
I had a girl; her name was Lize,
Chorus.
And she put whiskey in her pies,
Chorus.
Whiskey's gone, and I'll go too,
Chorus.
For without whiskey I can't do, etc.

A very enlivening windlass or pumping chant is I'm Bound for the Rio Grande:—

I'm bound away this very day,
  Oh, you Rio!
I'm bound away this very day,
  I'm bound for the Rio Grande!
And away, you Rio, oh, you Rio!
I'm bound away this ve-ry day,
  I'm bound for the Rio Grande!

Another is Homeward Bound with a Roaring Breeze:—

We're homeward bound with a roaring breeze,
  Good-by, fare you well!
We're homeward bound with a roaring breeze,
  Hurrah, my boys! We're homeward bound!

I wrote to Kitty, and she was well,
  Good-by, fare you well!
She rooms at the Astor and dines at the Bell,
  Hurrah, my boys! We're homeward bound!

There were many, with slight American variants, which were undoubtedly of English origin, and have been heard on English merchant ships from time immemorial; some which relate especially to the operations of whaling; and some which had their origin on the river flatboats and in the choruses of the roustabouts on the Ohio and Mississippi, and have been only slightly changed for salt-water purposes, the quality being as little varied as the number is endless. Their essential quality was that of an improvised chant, and the dominant feeling was to be found in the intermingling of the words and the cadence, as in the apparently meaningless refrain of the old ballads. They expressed, through all their rudeness and uncouthness, and more through the melody than the words, the minor chords which distinguish all folk music, the underlying element in the human heart oppressed by the magnitude and solitude of nature, as well as the enlivening spirit of strong exertion; and no sensitive ear could ever call them really gay, however vigorous and lively they might be. The shanties are passing away with the substitution of iron cranks and pulleys for the muscles of men, and the clank of machinery has taken the place of the melodious chorus from human throats. It is not probable that they will ever entirely disappear so long as men go down to the sea in ships;

but whatever life and flavor they had will fade away, and the first-class leading tenor among the "shanty men" will vanish with the need and appreciation of his skill. As for the old words, they will also be utterly lost, because they have no existence except in oral recitation and memory, and do not contain enough of the elements of pure poetry to secure their preservation in print, as the folk songs and ballads have been preserved. They are relics of custom rather than of literature; and although any poet or musician who deals with the sea will miss a source of very valuable inspiration if he does not possess himself of the spirit of their weird melody and the unconscious power of their vigorous rhythm, in themselves they are likely to be lost with the chants of the Phœnician sailors or the rowers of the galley of Ulysses, which they have succeeded, and some of whose melody they have perhaps reproduced.

The genuine sea songs differ from the shanties in that they had a definite poetical purpose to tell a story or express emotion, and were not merely words strung together to give voice to a rhythm of labor. It cannot be said that the genius of the American sailor has turned itself especially to expressing his emotions in song, any more than that of the English. His nature is entirely too practical, and the touch of tender sentiment which, in

There were many, with slight American variants, which were undoubtedly of English origin, and have been heard on English merchant ships from time immemorial; some which relate especially to the operations of whaling; and some which had their origin on the river flatboats and in the choruses of the roustabouts on the Ohio and Mississippi, and have been only slightly changed for salt-water purposes, the quality being as little varied as the number is endless. Their essential quality was that of an improvised chant, and the dominant feeling was to be found in the intermingling of the words and the cadence, as in the apparently meaningless refrain of the old ballads. They expressed, through all their rudeness and uncouthness, and more through the melody than the words, the minor chords which distinguish all folk music, the underlying element in the human heart oppressed by the magnitude and solitude of nature, as well as the enlivening spirit of strong exertion; and no sensitive ear could ever call them really gay, however vigorous and lively they might be. The shanties are passing away with the substitution of iron cranks and pulleys for the muscles of men, and the clank of machinery has taken the place of the melodious chorus from human throats. It is not probable that they will ever entirely disappear so long as men go down to the sea in ships;

but whatever life and flavor they had will fade away, and the first-class leading tenor among the "shanty men" will vanish with the need and appreciation of his skill. As for the old words, they will also be utterly lost, because they have no existence except in oral recitation and memory, and do not contain enough of the elements of pure poetry to secure their preservation in print, as the folk songs and ballads have been preserved. They are relics of custom rather than of literature; and although any poet or musician who deals with the sea will miss a source of very valuable inspiration if he does not possess himself of the spirit of their weird melody and the unconscious power of their vigorous rhythm, in themselves they are likely to be lost with the chants of the Phœnician sailors or the rowers of the galley of Ulysses, which they have succeeded, and some of whose melody they have perhaps reproduced.

The genuine sea songs differ from the shanties in that they had a definite poetical purpose to tell a story or express emotion, and were not merely words strung together to give voice to a rhythm of labor. It cannot be said that the genius of the American sailor has turned itself especially to expressing his emotions in song, any more than that of the English. His nature is entirely too practical, and the touch of tender sentiment which, in the Scotch nature, produced the beautiful fishing songs of the coast and the grand rowing and boat songs of the Western Islands, is wanting alike in him and his English associate.

It would probably astonish most readers to be told that English literature is singularly deficient in sea songs, when they have in memory the noble odes of Campbell, the long list of the Tom Bowlings and Jack Junks of Dibdin, Cherry's Bay of Biscay and The Minute Gun at Sea, and the many good songs about ships and sea fights by Barry Cornwall, Cunningham, and many others. But these songs were not written by sailors. There never has been any English sailor, except the respectable William Falconer, the author of The Shipwreck, in several cantos of desiccated decasyllabic verse, who has written of the sea in verse from the standpoint of actual experience, or to do for it in poetry what Captain Marryat, Michael Scott, and W. Clark Russell have done in prose. English sea songs have been written by landsmen; even the charming Wapping Old Stairs is a song of the waterside, and not of the ocean; and as for the famous heroes of Dibdin's nautical songs, including Tom Bowling himself, they are very much, as Thackeray said, "har-lar" Mr. T. P. Cooke, the actor, who personated the gallant Jack Tar in a very blue jacket with very bright buttons,

and very white duck trousers, and appealed to
"England, Home, and Beauty" as represented in
the cits of the gallery at Sadler's Wells theatre.
Dibdin's heroes smell of stage gas rather than of
tar, and their purpose and effect were very much
more to persuade susceptible landsmen that the
British navy was an elysium, in which beating
Frenchmen was a glorious episode in an existence
devoted mainly to passing the can between decks
at sea and basking in the smiles of lovely Nan and
faithful Poll on shore, than to tell what the seamen
themselves really felt about it. The writers of the
ordinary English sea songs had their lodgings in
the neighborhood of Drury Lane rather than in the
forecastle, and their inspiration was as strictly
commercial as that of Mr. Slum, who supplied the
anagrams and acrostics announcing the treasures
in Mrs. Jarley's waxworks. Some of them are
good in their way, as are a few of those of Dibdin
and Andrew Cherry, and particularly The Saucy
Arethusa, in which there is a real flavor of the sea
spirit, and which was written by one Prince Hoare,
a comic opera libretto writer of sixty years ago;
the author, by the way, of Mrs. Micawber's favorite song, Little Tafflin with the Silken Sash. But
when one comes to look for real forecastle songs,
written by a sailor, and smelling of pitch and tar,
one finds very few. Doubtless some have been

lost, although there is a strong vitality to anything that is good; but except Robert Kidd, Sailing down on the High Barbarie, Captain Glen, Jacky Tar with his Trousers on, — the immortal song which appealed to the feeling heart of Captain Edward Cuttle, —

> I know you would have me wed a farmer,
>   And not give me my heart's delight;
> Give me the lad whose tarry trousers
>   Shine to me like diamonds bright,—

The Mermaid, and few others, there is nothing which indicates that the British sailor was given to expressing himself in verse beyond the simple exigencies of the shanty. The case was very much the same with the American, and, under ordinary circumstances, it would be as vain to look for poetical feeling in the shrewd, practical-minded, and gritty New England seaman as in his more stolid and coarse-fibred English associate. Nevertheless, so much of the best spirit of the American people was once turned toward the sea for its field of action, its naval history has been so inspiring to national pride, and its record of adventure in all parts of the world has been so remarkable that it would have been impossible that it should not have produced some worthy or at least illustrative fruit in poetry.

The era of the Revolution was not distinguished

for its naval exploits, except the memorable raid of the Scotch adventurer, John Paul Jones, upon the English seas, and the fight of the Bonhomme Richard with the Serapis and the Countess of Scarborough, for the reason that the colonies had no warships, and no means of procuring any. There were, however, a few privateers: the Hyder Ali, commanded by Captain Barney, which won a victory over the British vessel General Monk, and was celebrated in verse by Philip Freneau, and for which he wrote a recruiting song, with at least one verse of a practical tendency:—

> Here's grog enough; come drink about.
> I know your hearts are firm and stout.
> American blood will never give out,
>   As often we have proved it;

the Fair American, commanded by Captain Daniel Hawthorne, which fought a British snow, laden with troops, off the coast of Portugal, and whose exploits are recorded in a ballad of very considerable spirit, and evidently by one of the crew; and some others, who did not happen to have a poet on board or a laureate on shore, and are not embalmed in verse. To this period, however, belongs what is, perhaps, the very best of American sea songs. We do not know whether its authorship was of that time or not, although it probably was, and from internal evidence would seem to have been composed by one of the very crew of the Ranger, Paul Jones's ship, which escaped from a British squadron in the Irish Channel in 1778. It was first published by Commodore Luce, in his collection of Naval Songs, with the statement that it was taken down from the recitation of a sailor. It is one of the gems of forecastle song, has the full scent of the brine and the gale, and the ship does not manœuvre as if she were a wagon on dry land, as was said of Allan Cunningham's account of Paul Jones's cruises. The title given is

THE YANKEE MAN-OF-WAR.

'T is of a gallant Yankee ship that flew the stripes and stars,
And the whistling wind from the west-nor'-west blew through the pitch-pine spars.
With her starboard tacks aboard, my boys, she hung upon the gale,
On an autumn night we raised the light on the old head of Kinsale.

It was a clear and cloudless night, and the wind blew steady and strong,
As gayly over the sparkling deep our good ship bowled along;
With the foaming seas beneath her bow the fiery waves she spread,
And bending low her bosom of snow, she buried her lee cathead.

There was no talk of short'ning sail by him who walked the poop,

And under the press of her pond'ring jib the boom bent like a hoop,
And the groaning water-ways told the strain that held her stout main tack.
But he only laughed as he glanced abaft at a white and silvery track.

The mid-tide meets in the channel waves that flow from shore to shore,
And the mist hung heavy upon the land from Featherstone to Dunmore;
And that sterling light on Tusker rock, where the old bell tolls the hour,
And the beacon light that shone so bright was quenched on Waterford tower.

The nightly robes onr good ship wore were her three topsails set,
The spanker and her standing jib, the spanker being fast.
"Now, lay aloft, my heroes bold, let not a moment pass!"
And royals and topgallant sails were quickly on each mast.

What looms upon the starboard bow? What hangs upon the breeze?
'Tis time our good ship hauled her wind abreast the old Saltees;
For by her ponderous press of sail and by her consorts four
We saw our morning visitor was a British man-of-war.

Up spoke our noble captain then, as a shot ahead of us passed,
"Haul snug your flowing courses, lay your topsail to the mast!"

The Englishmen gave three loud hurrahs from the deck of their covered ark,
And we answered back by a solid broadside from the decks of our patriot bark.

"Out, booms! Out, booms!" our skipper cried, "Out, booms, and give her sheet!"
And the swiftest keel that ever was launched shot ahead of the British fleet.
And amidst a thundering shower of shot, with stunsails hoisting away,
Down the North Channel Paul Jones did steer, just at the break of day.

The naval war of 1812 was a glorious epoch in American history. The achievements of the troops were very far from creditable, with a few exceptions, including, of course, the great one of the repulse of British regulars at New Orleans; but on the ocean the American sailors proved themselves quite the equal, if not more, of the English seamen, who had learned to consider themselves invincible, and despised the petty fleet of half a dozen cruisers, — not a single line-of-battle ship in the number, — which they had force enough to sweep off the seas without a struggle, and which they finally did blockade into inaction. There was quite an outburst of surprise, incredulity, and indignation in England, when the news came in that British frigates, one after another, the Guerriere, the Java, and the Macedonian, had been captured in single-ship fights by American ships of the same grade, and that in contests between vessels of smaller size, like the Wasp and the Frolic, the Hornet and the Peacock, Yankee pluck and seamanship had been equally successful; and British naval historians, then and since, have been earnest in showing that the victories were due to superior weight of metal, to the presence of deserters from the British navy on board the American ships, and to the accidents of naval warfare. Nevertheless, the facts of the captures remained the same, and privateers ravaged the seas, plundering and burning English ships, and causing the most bitter annoyance as well as incalculable loss and damage. To the vindictive depreciation and abuse of the English writers the Americans were not slow to respond, with a joyous outburst of national pride and exultation, and a mighty flapping of the wings of the American eagle; and the poets and song-writers joined in the shrill cock-a-doodle-doo of victory. The country was a great deal more boastful and self-assertive than it has been since it has come to rely on its own strength and has known the achievement of the great and sobering task of the civil war. The spirit of the spread eagle pervaded our national literature; the poets burst into songs, — generally, it must be admitted, very bad, — in which they celebrated the naval victories of the day. They indulged in mythological flights of the highest kind, in which Neptune bestowed a laurel crown upon Hull, Amphitrite smiled upon Bainbridge and Decatur, and the Tritons and the Nereids joined in a chorus of love and admiration for the American sailor. America, Commerce, and Freedom appeared as conjoined goddesses, and everybody was summoned to fill the bumper and pledge the flowing bowl, to thank the mighty Jove and invoke Bacchus, and do all sorts of things entirely unfamiliar to a people whose principal intoxicating beverages were Medford rum and Monongahela whiskey, and who had not the slightest acquaintance with heathen gods and goddesses. It is needless to say that none of these songs were written by sailors, or were ever sung by them, even if they could have been sung by anybody.

There was, however, better stuff than this in the naval songs of the war of 1812. The American sailor himself sometimes cleared his cheek of its quid, and sang in a clear if somewhat nasal voice some of the deeds which he had seen and done. Thus there is a great deal of rude vigor in one of the verses of a song describing the fight between the Constitution and the Guerriere, the first of our naval victories, and a very favorite theme:—

> But Jonathan kept cool,
> At the roaring of the Bull.

> His heart filled with anything but fears;
> And squirting out his quid,
> As he saw the captain did,
> He cleaned out his mouth for three cheers.

Another song on the same engagement, entitled Halifax Station, begins thus:—

> From Halifax Station a bully there came,
> To take or be taken, called Dacres by name;
> And who but a Yankee he met on his way;
> Says the Yankee to him, "Will you stop and take tea?"

After giving Dacres's high and mighty address to his crew, and Hull's more modest appeal, it says:—

> Then we off with our hats and gave him a cheer,
> Swore we'd stick by brave Hull, while a seaman could steer.
> Then at it we went with a mutual delight,
> For to fight and to conquer is a seaman's free right.

The poet naturally takes the privilege of presenting the confounded Britisher in the most humiliating light, and the manner in which Captain Dacres signified his surrender is probably more graphic than historically correct:—

> Then Dacres looked wild, and then sheathed his sword,
> When he found that his masts had all gone by the board.
> And, dropping astern, cries out to his steward,
> "Come up and be d——d! Fire a gun to leeward!"

This battle, fought in the North Atlantic on August

2, 1812, between the American frigate Constitution, Captain Isaac Hull, and the British frigate Guerriere, Captain James R. Dacres, and one of consummate seamanship as well as fighting capacity on the part of Hull, was the theme of the best and most spirited song of the whole war; one which still keeps its place in the forecastle, and, it may be hoped, will keep it so long as Uncle Sam has a war-ship afloat. It is set to a very lively and emphatic air, called, indifferently, The Landlady of France and The Bandy-Legged Officer, from the coarsely comical words which George Colman the younger had written to it.

THE CONSTITUTION AND THE GUERRIERE.

   It ofttimes has been told
   That the British sailors bold
Could flog the tars of France so neat and handy, O.
   And they never found their match
   Till the Yankees did them catch.
Oh, the Yankee boys for fighting are the dandy, O.

   The Guerriere, a frigate bold,
   On the foaming ocean rolled,
Commanded by proud Dacres, the grandee, O.
   With choice of British crew,
   As ever rammer drew,
They could flog the Frenchmen two to one so handy, O.

   When this frigate hove in view,
   Says proud Dacres to his crew,

"Come, clear the ship for action, and be handy, O.
  To the weather-gage, boys, get her,"
  And to make his men fight better
Gave them to drink gunpowder in their brandy, O.

  Then Dacres loudly cries,
  "Make this Yankee ship your prize!
You can in thirty minutes, neat and handy, O.
  Thirty-five's enough, I'm sure;
  And if you'll do it in a score,
I'll give you a double dose of brandy, O."

  The British shot flew hot,
  Which the Yankee answered not,
Till they got within the distance they called handy, O.
  Now says Hull unto his crew,
  "Boys, let's see what we can do.
If we take this boasting Briton, we're the dandy, O."

  The first broadside we poured
  Carried their mainmast by the board,
Which made the lofty frigate look abandoned, O.
  Then Dacres shook his head,
  And to his officers he said,
"Lord! I did n't think these Yankees were so handy, O."

  Our second told so well
  That their fore and mizzen fell,
Which doused the royal ensign so handy, O.
  "By George," says he, "we're done!"
  And he fired a lee gun,
While the Yankees struck up Yankee doodle dandy, O.

Then Dacres came on board
To deliver up his sword.
Loath was he to part with it, it was so handy, O.
"O, keep your sword," says Hull,
"For it only makes you dull.
So cheer up; let us take a little brandy, O."

Come, fill your glasses full,
And we'll drink to Captain Hull,
And so merrily will push about the brandy, O.
John Bull may toast his fill,
Let the world say what it will,
But the Yankee boys for fighting are the dandy, O.

The English celebrated their one signal victory of the war — the capture of the Chesapeake by the Shannon, off Boston Light, a year later — by a parody of this song, of a decidedly inferior quality.

One of the most notable events of the war was the cruise of the Essex, Captain David Porter, in the South Pacific, in 1813 and 1814. She did an immense amount of damage to the British whalemen, and the British ships Cherub and Phœbe were sent to capture her. After a rencontre in the harbor of Valparaiso, in which the captain of the Phœbe, taken at a disadvantage, protested his purpose to respect the neutrality of the port, and a challenge from which the British ships ran away, the Essex was caught disabled by a squall, chased into a harbor near Valparaiso, and captured after a tremendous engagement, in which the calibre of the British guns gave them every advantage, and in which the neutrality of the port was not taken into account. There was a poet on board the Essex, and he produced a long ballad describing the cruise and the retreat of the British ships after the challenge; but whether he perished in the later fight, or had no heart to add it to his verses, is not known. Among the crew of the Essex who did survive the fight was Midshipman David G. Farragut, who lived to achieve the greatest naval renown since that of Nelson, and be the theme of The Bay Fight, the noblest sea poem yet written.

The ballad of the Essex is entitled " A Pleasant New Song. Chanted by Nathan Whiting (through his nose) for the amusement of the galley slaves on board the Phœbe, who are allowed to sing nothing but psalms." After describing the beginning of the trouble caused by " John Bull's taking our ships and kidnaping our true sailors," and the capture of British vessels in the first year of the war, the ballad takes up the cruise of the Essex.

> The saucy Essex, she sailed out
>   To see what she could do.
> Her captain is from Yankee land,
>   And so are all her crew.
>
> Away she sailed, so gay and trim,
>   Down to the Galapagos,

And toted all the terrapins,
    And nabbed the slippery whalers.

And where d' ye think we next did go?
    Why, down to the Marquesas.
And there we buried underground
    Some thousand golden pieces.

Then sailed about the ocean wide,
    Sinking, burning, taking,
Filling pockets, spilling oil,
    While Johnny's heart was aching.

The ballad then describes the arrival of the Phœbe and Cherub and the rencontre in Valparaiso Bay, the challenge and the flight of the Phœbe, in verses which have a great deal of rude vigor.

At last John Bull quite sulky grew,
    And called us traitors all,
And swore he 'd fight our gallant crew,
    Paddies and Scots and all.

Then out he went in desperate rage,
    Swearing, as sure as day,
He 'd starve us all or dare us out
    Of Valparaiso Bay.

Then out he sailed in gallant trim,
    As if he thought to fright us,
Run up his flag and fired a gun
    To say that he would fight us.

Our cables cut, we put to sea,
    And ran down on his quarter,

And Johnny clapped his helm hard up,
    And we went following after.

In haste to join the Cherub he
    Soon bent his scurvy way,
While we returned in merry glee
    To Valaparaiso Bay.

And let them go. To meet the foe
    We 'll take no farther trouble,
Since all the world must fairly know
    They 'll only fight us double.

Ne'er mind, my lads, let 's drink and sing,
    " Free trade and sailors' rights."
May liquor never fail the lad
    Who for his country fights.

Huzza, my lads, let 's drink and sing,
    And toast them as they run :
" Here 's to the sailors and their king
    Who 'll fight us two to one."

There were other exploits of American ships told in verse, among them the gallant repulse, by the crew of the privateer General Armstrong, Captain Samuel C. Reid, in the Harbor of Fayal, of the boats of three British men-of-war, which was the subject of a forecastle ballad, but none of this memorial verse reached the level of poetry. The battles of Lake Erie and Lake Champlain also had their numerous laureates; and the raid of Admiral Cockburn and the troops upon Baltimore was the subject of a song, the opening lines of which have a vigor and strong rhythm not maintained throughout.

> Old Ross, Cochrane, and Cockburn too,
>   And many a bloody villain more,
> Swore with their bloody, savage crew
>   That they would plunder Baltimore.

The naval service during the civil war did not produce any songs that achieved popularity in comparison with that won by the songs of land service, like John Brown's Body, The Year of Jubilo, and Marching through Georgia, and in fact was singularly deficient in poetry, with the remarkable exception of the productions of Mr. Henry Howard Brownell. There were few single-ship engagements except the fight between the Monitor and the Merrimac, and the Kearsarge and the Alabama, and the blockading service was not calculated to inspire the martial muse.

The two great naval achievements of the war were the capture of New Orleans and of the forts in Mobile Bay by the fleets under Farragut; and these were celebrated in poetry worthy of them — and no more can be said — by Henry Howard Brownell, who witnessed the second from the deck of Admiral Farragut's flagship. The fire, spirit, and grand fighting *élan* of The Bay Fight have never been surpassed in English poetry, and the accuracy of its pictures is as notable as their vigor. But these are poems, and not songs, and there is nothing in the naval songs of the civil war which will compare with those of the war of 1812. It was rather past the time for the genuine forecastle ballad, and none of the land poets hit the true vein, as Buchanan Read, Stedman, and others did when commemorating military exploits.

There was one other field of American seamanship, full of romance and excitement, which should have produced some worthy poetry and song, and that was the whaling service before the days of iron steamers and bomb lances. The chase of the gigantic cetacean in the lonely solitude of the Arctic and Indian oceans, the fights in frail boats with the maddened monster and all the perils of sea and storm, the visits to the palmy islands in the Southern Sea and the frozen solitude of the Arctic, were full of the materials of poetry. The long watches of the monotonous cruising during the four years' voyage gave plenty of time for any occupation, whether it was carving whales' teeth or making verses; and there were many bright spirits, attracted by the adventure of whaling, who could have made a literary use of their opportunity. The novels of Herman Melville, some of the strongest and most original in our literature, have given the romance of the South Sea islands as they appeared to the adventurer of that day; and in Moby Dick, or The White Whale, he has shown both the prose and the poetry of a whaling cruise with singular power, although with some touch of extravagance at the end. The whaling songs are, however, not very abundant, nor, it must be confessed, of a high standard of quality. To this there is one remarkable exception, which appears to be wholly unknown in American literature, although it has been in print. It is entitled a "Brand Fire New Whaling Song Right from the Pacific Ocean. Tune, Maggy Lander. By a Foremast Hand," and was printed in a little five-cent pamphlet, by E. B. Miller, in New Bedford, in 1831. It does not seem to have come under the eye of any critic who could appreciate its spirit and faithfulness, and no mention is made of it in any of the collections of American poetry. It is extremely doubtful if the author received enough from its sale to repay him for the investment of a portion of his " lay " in printing it, and his name is utterly lost in his modest pseudonym of " Foremast Hand;" so that he obtained neither fame nor fortune from his epic. The poem, which is too long for entire quotation, was unquestionably the work of a sailor on a whaling ship, and probably, as he says, of a foremast hand. It lacks some of the finish of professional literature, as shown in the ruggedness of some of its rhymes, and the vigorous compulsion of the rules of grammar and syntax, when necessary, although the author was evidently of higher education than would belong to one in his position, and its jigging measure becomes tiresome; but it is of very great spirit and vigor, as well as fidelity to its theme, and by no means deserves to have fallen so entirely into oblivion. Indeed, it seems to me to be quite as good as, and a great deal more original than, any American poetry which had appeared up to that time. The song has for its subject the chase and capture of a whale in the North Pacific, and relates the course of events from the time of the first sighting of "white water" on the horizon by the lookouts to that when the monster, stabbed to death by the keen lances, rolls "fins out" in the bloody water, amid the hurrahs of the excited boats' crews. All the details of this *grande chasse* are given with wonderful vigor, as well as faithfulness, and the historian of the whale fishery will find it as accurate as a log-book. Perhaps the account of the chase by the boats and the harpooning will give as good an idea of the force and spirit of the poem as any part of it; and, in reference to the emphasis of the language, it may be remembered that mates of whaling ships in pursuit of an eight-hundred-barrel whale had a good deal of energy and excitement to relieve. The boats have been lowered, and are darting toward the unsuspecting whale with all the speed of ashen oars and vigorous muscle, while their commanders objurgate and stimulate the crews, as the poet says, "judiciously."

"Pull, men, for, lo, see there they blow !
   They 're going slow as night, too.
Pull, pull, you dogs ! they lie like logs, —
   Thank Heaven they 're headed right, too."

. . . .

"The chance is ours ! " the mate now roars.
   "Spring, spring, nor have it said, men,
That we could miss a chance like this
   To take them head and head, men.
There 's that old *sog*, he 's like a log.
   Spring, lads, and show your mettle ;
Strain every oar ; let 's strike before
   He 's *gallied, mill,* or *settle.*"

And so it is, the chance is his.
   The others peak their oars now.
From his strained eyes the lightning flies,
   And lion-like he roars now.
"Pull, pull, my lads ! why don't you pull ?
   For God's sake, pull away, men !
Hell's blazes ! pull but three strokes more,
   And we have won the day, men !

" Stand up there, forward — pull the rest —
   Hold water — give it to her !

> Stern all, stern all — God damn it, heave
>   Your other iron through her !
> We're fast, we're fast — stern out her way !
>   Here, let me come ahead, men.
> There, peak your oars — wet — line — wet — line —
>   Why, bloody zounds, you're dead, men !"

The rush of the whale towing the boat, his sounding to the uttermost length of the line, his reappearance, the lancing, the mad dash at the boats, and the death flurry are all described with great vividness, but there is room only for the verses in which the monster comes up from his long dive, and obliges the poet to appeal to the enemy of sea songs, the steam boiler: —

> Till from the deep, with mighty leap,
>   Full length the monster breaches, —
> So strongly sped, his scarred gray head
>   High as our topmast reaches ;
> And, like a rock, with startling shock,
>   From mountain height descending,
> Down thunders he upon the sea,
>   Ocean with ether blending.
>
> And, hark ! once more that lengthened roar,
>   As from his spout-hole gushing,
> His breath, long spent, now finds a vent,
>   Like steam from boiler rushing.

It does not seem that a poet who could write so vividly and forcefully as this ought to be without a place in American literature, even if there were no other interest in his work.

There is another whaling song, entitled The Coast of Peru, and undoubtedly the work of a forecastle poet, which is worth preserving, despite its homeliness, for its genuine flavor, and as a relic of the old days before steam whalers and bomb lances took so much of the romance out of the fishery.

THE COAST OF PERU.

Come, all ye bold sailors,
    Who sail 'round Cape Horn,
Come, all the bold whalers,
    Who cruise 'round for sperm.
The Captain has told us,
    And I hope 't will prove true
That there's plenty of sperm whales
    Off the coast of Peru.

The first whale we saw
    Near the close of the day.
Our Captain came on deck,
    And thus he did say:
"Now all my bold sailors,
    Pray be of good glee,
For we'll see him in the morning,
    P'raps under our lee."

It was early next morning,
    Just as the sun rose,
The man at the mast-head
    Called out, "There she blows!"

"Whereaway?" cried our Captain,
    As he sprang up aloft.
"Three points on our lee bow,
    And scarce two miles off."

"Now trace up your yards, boys,
    We'll fasten anear.
Get your lines in your boats,
    See your box lines all clear;
Haul back the main yard, boys,
    Stand by, each boat's crew,
Lower away, lower away,
    My brave fellows, do."

"Now, bend to your oars, boys,
    Just make the boat fly,
But whatever you do, boys,
    Keep clear from his eye."
The first mate soon struck,
    And the whale he went down,
While the old man pulled up,
    And stood by to bend on.

But the whale soon arose;
    To the windward he lay.
We hauled up 'longside,
    And he showed us fair play.
We caused him to vomit,
    Thick blood for to spout,
And in less than ten minutes
    We rolled him "fin out."

We towed him alongside
    With many a shout,

>   That day cut him in,
>   And began to boil out.
>   Oh, now he's all boiled out
>   And stowed down below,
>   We're waiting to hear 'em,
>   Sing out, "There she blows!"

It is extremely doubtful if the Dago sailors and foreign 'longshoremen, who now make such a large portion of the crews of the Arctic steam whalers, are capable of even such rude verse as this, and the poetry of the whale fishery is now as extinct as the glory of Nantucket and the sea flavor of New Bedford. Like some greater things it may be regretted, but cannot be recovered.

FOLK-SONGS OF THE CIVIL WAR.

OF collections and criticisms of the songs and poetry of the civil war in this country there is no lack. Newspaper files and popular song-books have been ransacked, as well as more pretentious volumes, and whatever possessed a modicum of what is termed "poetic merit" has been gathered with pious care. The standard in most cases has, naturally enough, been that of "polite literature," that of which the writers were persons of education, and who endeavored to express with more or less force a dominant sentiment in logical as well as grammatical form, and to embody their meaning in intelligent words. If popular songs, which did not fulfil these conditions, have been included, it has usually been with an apology for their uncouthness, or a contemptuous reference to their banality, and an intimation that they were forced into the pages of the collection, or upon the attention of the critic, because they could not be ignored in any representative collection of the poetry of the war. Nevertheless, it may be doubted if these uncouth rhymes, without sense or consecutive meaning, like Dixie's Land and John Brown's Body, or the cheap sentimentality of Just before the Battle, Mother, and When this Cruel War is over, do not have something of the indefinable fascination on the printed page which they had to the ears of the men who sung them, and do not take a stronger hold upon the mind than the much more elegant and refined verses by which they are surrounded. Something of this may be due to the memory of those who heard them, and in whose minds they were the voice of the war, as the flags, the arms, and the uniforms were its visible insignia, but this does not entirely account for their fascination and permanence. There was something about them which endowed them with vital life, which gave them a hold upon every tongue and upon every heart, a quality distinct from obvious meaning, to say nothing of literary excellence, and which can only be described as the singing element. It was to accomplish this purpose, to relieve the heart through the lungs, without reference to the mind, to emphasize and lighten the buoyant or weary march, and give voice to the pervading impulse, which kept these songs alive and made them a practical part of the war, as the sailor's "shanties" were a part of the life of the sea, and the negro choruses of the life of the plantation. This fascination may fade when the civil war becomes a matter of distant history, and John

Brown's Body be no more than a set of unmeaning jingles to future generations, as Lillibullero, which "sung King James out of three kingdoms," is to our own; but with their death will come a loss of a vital element of the war, as representing its living and human sentiment, and history will miss its function if it exclude them. How vital they were at the time may be seen from the fact that the attempts to supersede the unmeaning rhymes by words of substance and definite poetry had no effect, so far as their popular use was concerned, even when this was done with such magnificent success as in Mrs. Julia Ward Howe's Battle Hymn of the Republic, or General Albert Pike's powerful lines to Dixie. The people and the soldiers clung to the old choruses, and passed by with cold respect or indifference the deliberate and purely literary appeals to their feelings. There is, perhaps, a reason for this, which may be accounted for under the canons of literary criticism. A song is something different from a poem, and includes a dominant appeal to the ear, which may be even obstructed by elaborate meaning, and the simple and taking air is the essential thing. It is not always the case that a popular or national song is meaningless, as is shown in the Marseillaise and Der Wacht am Rhein; and, in our own war, Mr. James R. Randall's My Maryland was as popular in the Southern army as a song as it is vigorous and spirited as a piece of pure literature. But as a whole, songs which have been sung by large bodies of men, under stress of high excitement, have depended more upon their sound than their meaning for their vogue, and this would doubtless apply to the chants of the Crusaders as to the choruses of the Northern and Southern soldiers during the civil war. God save the King does not compare with Ye Mariners of England in any element of poetry, yet the one is always sung and the latter never; and Marching through Georgia depends upon its air rather than its commonplace words for its hold upon the martial heart. There was some good poetry written during the late civil war, although not much; and in the collections, as I have said, it is doubtful if the respectable verses, in which the incidents and feelings of the war were expressed with deliberate art, have the vitality, as they have not now the effect, of the rude rhymes and commonplace sentimentality of those songs which took hold of the hearts of the people, and were the living voices of the war. Too often they had the contortions of patriotism without its inspiration, and were forcible-feeble in appeal, or, when they attempted to interpret the spirit of battle, rang false to the real feeling and knowledge of the soldier. To this there were brilliant exceptions, like Mr. Gibbons's We are coming, Father Abraham, Mr. Henry Howard Brownell's naval poems, and Read's Sheridan's Ride, but as a whole it must be confessed that the polite poetry of the civil war is rather dreary reading.

There was an immense amount of song-writing as well as of song-singing during the war, and under the stress of excitement and the gathering together of immense bodies of young and exuberant spirits the enthusiasm inevitably found a vent through the lungs. The illiterate poets were as busy as those of higher education; and those who did not seek their public through the pages of the fashionable magazine, or even the poet's corner of the country newspaper, but through the badly printed sheet of the penny street ballad, or through the mouth of the negro minstrel, contributed almost as largely to the poetry of the war as their brothers. Dime song-books containing a curious admixture of the common and the polite, the appropriate and the incongruous, were innumerable, and the poetry which is below literary criticism was equal in bulk to that which is within its scope. Actual soldiers and sailors also sometimes wrote of their battles and experiences, or expressed their feelings in more or less finished verse, and these found their way into print either in the ballad sheet or the newspaper. Most of those which were good in themselves, from their native force and vigor or from their power as songs, have been preserved, but there is an immense amount of this uncollected and unedited verse which has a very great value as illustrating the sentiments and condition of the people, the waves of popular feeling during various phases of the war, the impressions of notable incidents and the estimates of prominent personages, and which tell, oftentimes more than the leading articles in the newspapers, how the common people were affected by the tremendous struggle. They have the interest, if no other, of the relics of arms and uniforms, and the tokens of the familiar life of a bygone age, and will one day be as valuable to the historian as the ballads of the civil war in England, which have been collected with so much care. In modern times and in civilized societies, the newspaper has taken the place of the street ballad as the record of historical events and the expression of political feeling, and Ireland is almost the only country where it now lingers in any quantity and force; but during such times of popular excitement, and the occurrence of great events involving the most intimate interests of the people, as during the civil war, the popular ballads resumed something of their former value as the expressions of popular feeling. It would be a mistake to omit from consideration even those which were provided as a matter of professional business by the minstrels of the popular stage, who reflected the pervading sentiments of the time, and colored their rude comedy and cheap pathos with the thoughts and feelings aroused by the war.

Thousands of these street songs were issued, to have their temporary vogue and disappear. The principal publisher of the penny sheets was H. de Marsan, 34 Chatham Street, New York, and he appears to have had almost a monopoly of the trade. They were printed on coarse paper, with an emblematic border in colors representing the American flag, and with a soldier and sailor under arms. Some of the more successful songs were copyrighted and published with their music, but this appears to have made little difference to the enterprising Chatham Street publisher, for he included almost everything that was singable, old Revolutionary ballads, English naval songs, and some of the more finished American poems of the war, as well as Ethiopian melodies, and ballads obviously of original contribution. It would be interesting to know whether he kept a staff of poets, like Jemmy Catnach of Seven Dials, or whether, as is most probable, he simply took what he could find, and conferred the honors of print, without remuneration, upon voluntary contributors. The most numerous contributors who bear the stamp of originality naturally came from the Irish element in New York, who were familiar with the street ballad at home, and reproduced its form and sentiment for a similar audience. There are dozens of ballads relating to the exploits of the Sixty-Ninth Regiment, an Irish organization in the New York State Guard, of which Michael Corcoran, an ex-member of the Irish constabulary, was colonel, and Thomas Francis Meagher, the Irish revolutionist, and afterward a brigadier-general of volunteers, a captain. The regiment took part in the battle of Bull Run, during which Colonel Corcoran was taken prisoner and carried South. The bards were instantly inspired to sing the praises of the regiment and its commander, and ballads were written exactly reproducing the style and language of the Irish " Come, all yez," as thus : —

Come, all ye Gallant Heroes, along with me combine ;
I'll sing to you a ditty about the Glorious Sixty-Ninth.
They are a band of Brothers, from Ireland they came ;
They had a bold Commander, Michael Corcoran was his
    name.

In one or two of them there is an improvement on this very primitive verse, gleams of humor and ebullitions of vigorous spirit. A song entitled The Jolly Sixty-Ninth has a rollicking rhythm and rude humor, of which the following is a specimen : —

It happened one fine day,
Down by the rajin say,
Quite convenient to the boilin' Gulf of Mexico,
That some chaps hauled down our flag,
And it through the dust did drag,
Swearin' it should never float on Fort Sumpter, O.

The author of a song entitled Freedom's Guide had a force and vigor which, with a little more polish and form, would have entitled him to a place in polite literature, and the real singable quality, which was, perhaps, of more importance: —

FREEDOM'S GUIDE.

Our country now is great and free,
And this forever it shall be.
 We know the way — we know the way.
Though Southern foes may gather here,
We will protect what we hold dear.
 We know the way.

Chorus. We know the way — we know the way.
 Through Baltimore, hooray.
 For our guide is Freedom's banner.
  Hooray, hooray.
 The way is through Baltimore.

The South shall see that we are true,
And that we know a thing or two.
 We know the way — we know the way.
As Yankee boys we are at hand,
Our countless throngs shall fill the land.
 We know the way.

From east to west, from south to north,
We'll send our mighty legions forth.
   We know the way — we know the way.
The freedom that our fathers won
Shall be defended by each son.
   We know the way.

Then shout, then shout o'er hill and plain,
We will our country's rights maintain.
   We know the way — we know the way.
We will always guard it with our might,
And keep steadfast in the right.
   We know the way.

Old Jeff has now begun to lag,
He knows that we'll stand by the flag.
   We know the way — we know the way.
With Scott to guide us in the right,
We'll show them how the Sixty-Ninth can fight.
   We know the way.

An organization almost equally popular with the New York ballad singers, in the early days of the war, was the "Fire Zouaves," recruited among the firemen of the metropolis, and which was expected to perform wonderful feats of daring and energy, from the character of its material. Its leader, Colonel Elmer E. Ellsworth, was killed by the landlord of a hotel in Alexandria, Va., while hauling down the rebel flag from the roof, and his death created a deep sensation from its dramatic character, and from the fact that it was among the earliest in the war. The elegies upon his death were numerous, as well as those in praise of the regiment itself. One of the latter, by Archibald Scott, whose name, contrary to the usual custom, was prefixed to the ballad, had a good deal of rude vigor, of which the following is a specimen:—

> Shall ugly plugs of Baltimore,
> Who come out with stones and staves,
> Get leave our patriots' blood to pour,
> And drive our soldiers from their shore?
> No, no! by Hell, in flames shall roar
> Their city first by York Zouaves!

Another phase of life in the cities, from that of the enthusiasm of the young men in marching to the war and the fervent appeals for enlistment, was that of the feelings of the women whose sons and husbands left their workshops to join the army. The grief was as bitter and the patriotism as sincere among the inmates of the crowded tenement houses and the narrow and barren homes of the families of the workingmen of New York as among their sisters in the farmhouses in the country, whose surroundings better lent themselves to the illumination of poetry, and it cost as much to put down the tin pail of the city laborer as for the farmer to

> Lay down the axe, fling by the spade,

and even more in pinching poverty and lack of resource. But the griefs and sacrifices of these women of the city tenement and noisome alley have found no place in the genteel poetry of the war, and have only been expressed in the rude verse of the street ballad. Says one of them: —

> It was in the month of April,
>   As I walked out one day,
> I met a woman weeping
>   As I walked down Broadway.
> She was weeping for her Johnny,
>   Her dear and only son,
> Who joined the Northern army
>   To fight in Washington.
> O Johnny! I gave you a schoolin',
>   I gave you a trade likewise,
> And when you joined the Volunteers,
>   You know 't was my advice."

The New York ballad writers were not entirely confined to the English language, the large foreign population furnishing recruits of all nations. There is not, so far as I have seen, any original German song devoted to the Union cause, but The Red, White, and Blue, and other patriotic songs, were published in German text; and of Germanized-English songs, most if not all the product of variety theatre performers, there were a great many, including the extremely popular I'm going to fight mit Siegel.

Ven I comes from de Deutsche Countree,
　I vorks somedimes at baking.
Den I keeps a lager bier saloon,
　And den I goes shoemaking.
But now I vas a sojer man
　To save the Yankee eagle,
To SCHLAUCH dem dam Southern folks,
　I'm going to fight mit Siegel.

But this was no more representative of German sentiments than the "Whack-row-de-dow" Pats of the stage were of the Irish; and the German soldiers, when they sang in the vernacular, enlivened their foreign patriotism with the songs of the Fatherland. There was at least one French poet who appealed to his countrymen in their own language to rally to the cause of the Union. His production was as follows:—

VENGEONS LA PATRIE.

HYMNE PATRIOTIQUE, PAR GUSTAVE DIME, OUVRIER-ESTAMPEUR: AIR, "GLOIRE AUX MARTYRS VICTORIAUX."

APPEL AUX ARMES.

Debout fils de l'Union
　Pour venges l'infamie
Faite à la nation,
　Pour venger la Patrie,
La Constitution !
A bas Rébellion !

Debout, debout Américains,
Debout les armes à main.

L'OUTRAGE.

De Baltimore à Charleston,
   De Richmont à Montgomery,
Le grand drapeau de Washington
   Partout il fut souillie, flétri,
Du Fort Sumpter vengeons l'outrage
   Et en la sol de Virginie
Sachions montrer notre courage
   En digne fils de la Patrie.

L'ASSASSINAT.

Le Sud in horrible furie
   DU POIGNARD DE LA TRAHISON
Perçant le cœur de la Patrie,
   Proclame à la SECESSION.
Mais le President héroique
   Et l'Autorité, le Sénat,
Sauront sauver la République
   Et cet infame Assassinat.

LE TRIOMPHE.

Gloire à ton nom, libre Amérique,
   Gloire à tes vaillant défenseurs
Ils sauveront la République,
   Terrasseront tes oppresseurs.
Ils volent tous à la victoire,
   Pour l'Union des Etats Unis.
Ils reviendront couverts de gloire
   Et les traitres SERONT PUNIS.

The "ouvrier-estampeur" was sufficiently energetic, but his song never became the Franco-American Marseillaise.

As the war dragged its slow length along, demanding greater and greater sacrifices, and with its days of repulse and defeat for the Union armies, the feeling of universal enthusiasm gave way to discouragement, and there were not wanting in New York, among its heterogeneous population, elements of bitterness which culminated in the deadly and shameful outbreak of the draft riots. This feeling manifested itself in the street ballads, not so conspicuously as the previous enthusiasm, but enough to have attracted the attention of those who were watching the signs of popular feeling. "Copperheadism" had its bards as well as loyalty, although they were much fewer in number, and they cannot be omitted in an account of the folk-songs of the civil war. A rude jingle entitled Johnny, fill up the Bowl, gave the popular expression to this feeling: —

> Abram Lincoln, what yer 'bout?
> Hurrah, hurrah.
> Stop this war, for it's played out,
> Hurrah, hurrah.
>
> Abram Lincoln, what yer 'bout?
> Stop this war, for it's played out.

We'll all drink stone-blind,
Johnny fill up the bowl.

The pages of the dime song-books at this time contained a number of songs in opposition to the draft, expressing hatred to the negro, and a demand for the stoppage of the war, of which the following is an example: —

THE BEAUTIES OF CONSCRIPTION.

And this the "people's sovereignty,"
 Before a despot humbled,
Lies in the dust 'neath power unjust,
 With crown and sceptre crumbled.
Their brows distained — like felons chained
 To negroes called "their betters,"
Their whinings drowned in "Old John Brown,"
 Poor *sovereigns* wearing fetters.
  Hurrah for the Conscription,
   American Conscription !
  Well have they cashed old Lincoln's drafts,
   Hurrah for the Conscription !

Some think the hideous spectacle
 Should move the heart to sadness,
That fetters ought — oh silly thought ! —
 Sting freemen's hearts to madness.
When has the stock of Plymouth rock
 Been melted to compunction ?
As for Provos, the wide world knows
 That chaining is their function.
  Hurrah for the Conscription,
   American Conscription,

And for the stock of Plymouth rock,
   Whence sprung this new Conscription !

What matter if you 're *sandwiched* in
  A host of sable fellows,
Well flavored men, your kith and kin,
  As Abe and Sumner tell us ?
Is not the war — this *murder* — for
  The negro, *nolens volens ?*
For every three now killed of ye
  There 's just a negro stolen.
    And then ye have Conscription,
    American Conscription,
    Your blood must flow for this, you know.
    Hurrah for the Conscription !

The songs written by the soldiers and sailors themselves, descriptive of their engagements, or incidents of camp and march, or expressing their feelings, were not many, either in folk-ballads or finished poetry. Major J. W. De Forrest's powerful verses, In Louisiana, are almost the only specimen of the latter, and there are but few of the ruder ballads. It may have been because the soldiers and sailors were too much occupied, and that the life in camp and on shipboard was not favorable to poetical reverie, although there were many hours on picket or watch which might have been thus employed; but the fact remains that there was more carving of bone rings than of verses, and more singing than writing in the army and navy. There was not an absolute dearth, however, and the soldiers and sailors sometimes told their own stories or expressed their own feelings in verse. One of the best of these was written during the early days of the war by H. Millard, a member of Company A, Seventy-first Regiment, concerning the march from Annapolis to the Junction, and has the genuine flavor of soldiership as well as a fine spirit of *camaraderie*. It is entitled Only Nine Miles to the Junction: —

    The Rhode Island boys were posted along
        On the road from Annapolis station,
    As the Seventy-first Regiment, one thousand strong,
        Went on in defense of the nation.
    We 'd been marching all day in the sun's scorching ray,
        With two biscuits each as a ration,
    When we asked Gov. Sprague to show us the way,
        And " How many miles to the Junction ? "
        How many miles — how many miles,
            And how many miles to the Junction ;
        When we asked Gov. Sprague to show us the way,
            And " How many miles to the Junction ? "

    The Rhode Island boys cheered us on out of sight,
        After giving the following injunction :
    " Just keep up your courage, you 'll come out all right,
        For it 's only nine miles to the Junction."
    They gave us hot coffee, a grasp of the hand,
        Which cheered and refreshed our exhaustion ;

> We reached in six hours the long-promised land,
>   For 't was only nine miles to the Junction.

There were not many attempts to describe the battles in which the soldiers took part, and they were left to the poets, who did not see them, and had to depend, not very successfully, upon their imagination. There was, however, a ballad of the Seven Days' Fight before Richmond, evidently written by a soldier, and of some force and vigor. It begins: —

> Away down in old Virginny many months ago,
> McClellan made a movement and made it very slow.
> The Rebel Generals found it out and pitched into our rear;
> They caught the very devil, for they found old Kearney
>   there.
>   In the old Virginny low-lands, low-lands,
>   The old Virginny low-lands, low.

The bard details the fights as though they were a succession of Union victories, and concludes with a defense of General McClellan: —

> Now all you politicians, a word I have for you,
> Just let our little Mac alone, for he is tried and true;
> For you have found out lately that he is our only hope,
> For twice he saved the Capitol, likewise McDowell and
>   Pope.

The enthusiasm aroused by General McClellan among the rank and file of the Army of the Potomac had no counterpart in regard to any other commander, was proof against failure and defeat, and lingered, to a certain extent, even to the close of the war. His removal caused a great deal of indignation, and called out a good many protests and appeals for his restoration. A song, Give us back our old Commander, was a good deal sung at the time: —

> Give us back our old Commander,
>   Little Mac, the people's pride ;
> Let the army and the nation
>   In their choice be satisfied.
> With McClellan as our leader,
>   Let us strike the blow anew ;
> Give us back our old Commander,
>   He will see the battle through.
>   Give us back our old Commander,
>   Let him manage, let him plan ;
>   With McClellan as our leader,
>   We can wish no better man.

The very rollicking and nonsensical chorus of Bummers, come and meet Us, belongs to this period, and was almost as popular as John Brown's Body, fulfilling amply and simply the conditions for relieving the lungs. Like the sailors' "shanties" and the plantation choruses, it was capable of indefinite extension and improvisation. The following is a specimen of its construction : —

McClellan is our leader, we've had our last retreat,
McClellan is our leader, we've had our last retreat,
McClellan is our leader, we've had our last retreat,
  We'll now go marching on.

 Say, brothers, will you meet us,
 Say, brothers, will you meet us,
 Say, brothers, will you meet us,
  As we go marching on?

. . . .

The girls we left behind us, boys, our sweethearts in the North,
The girls we left behind us, boys, our sweethearts in the North,
The girls we left behind us, boys, our sweethearts in the North,
  Smile on us as we march.

 Oh sweethearts, don't forget us,
 Oh sweethearts, don't forget us,
 Oh sweethearts, don't forget us,
  We'll soon come marching home.

A seaman on board the Vandalia, one of the ships engaged in the capture of Port Royal, wrote a description of the engagement, which has considerable of the light of battle in it. It is entitled: —

THE PORT ROYAL DANCE.

Behold our glorious banner floats gayly in the air,
But four hours hence base traitors swore we could not plant it there;

But brave Dupont he led us on to fight the vaunting foe,
And soon the rebel standard was in the dust laid low.
   Whack row de dow,
    How are you, old Port Royal?
   Whack row de dow,
    How are you, Secesh?

When we were seen advancing they laughed with foolish pride,
And said that soon our Northern fleet they'd sink beneath the tide;
And with their guns trained carefully they waited our advance,
And the gallant Wabash soon struck up the music of the dance.

The Susquehanna next in line delivered her broadside,
With deadly aim each shot was sent and well each gun was plied;
And still our gallant ships advanced, and each one, as she passed,
Poured in her deadly messengers, and the foe fell thick and fast.

Each ship advanced in order, each captain wore a smile,
Until the famed Vandalia brought up the rear in style,
And as our guns were shortest we balanced to the right,
And brought us to the enemy the closest in the fight.

Then round the room (Port Royal bay) we took a Highland Fling,
And showed them in Fort Walker what loud music we could sing.
And then we poured in our broadsides that brought their courage low,
And o'er the rebel batteries soon our Union flag did flow.

Three cheers for gallant Haggerty, he led us safely through;
And three for our loved Whiting, he is the real true blue.
Success to every officer who fought with us that day;
Together may we pass unscathed through many a gallant
    fray.

A health to every gallant tar who did his duty well,
Peace to the ashes of the dead who nobly fighting fell.
'T was in a glorious cause they died, the Union to maintain.
We who are left, when called upon, will try it o'er again.

Some of the disagreeable features of a soldier's duty and camp life were dealt with by the soldiers in the spirit of humorous exaggeration, which was as much an evidence of high spirits as the enthusiastic choruses. A camp poet thus relieves his feelings in regard to the exercise of " double quick: " —

Since I became a volunteer things have went rather queer;
Some say I'm a three months' man, and others a three years'
    volunteer.
With plenty of likes and dislikes to all I have to stick;
There's plenty of pork, salt horse, and plenty of Double-
    Quick.
        Oh, I'm miserable, I'm miserable,
          To all I'll have to stick.
        The old salt horse is passable,
          But d———n the Double-Quick.

If a friend should call to see you the men have a pretty game.
They call him paymaster, obstacle, or some such kind of a
    name.

They chase him around the camp; it's enough to make him sick
To try and teach him discipline by giving him Double-Quick.

You may feel rather hungry, almost in a starving state,
And you wish to get your dinner first, all ready with your plate;
There's always others just the same, waiting for the lick;
To be the twentieth one, you must travel Double-Quick.

Once upon every Sunday to church you must always go,
Your bayonet by your side in case you should meet the foe;
And when the service was ended it was called the moral trick
To drive you back to your camp at a pleasant Double-Quick.

Each day there are just twelve roll-calls to keep you in the camp;
If off three rods the bugle sounds, back you will have to tramp,
And, if you chance to miss, why, you are a poor, gone chick,—
Fourteen bricks in your knapsack, and four hours Double-Quick.

Now, all you chaps who would enlist, don't leap before you look,
And, if you wish to fight for the Union, go on your own hook,
For, if a soldier you become, it will be your last kick,
To the devil you will surely be drove headlong Double-Quick.

The Southern poetry of the civil war was even more rhetorical and stilted than that of the North. Its literary culture was more provincial, and its style a great deal more inflated and artificial. It was the "foemen" that they were to meet instead of the enemy, and "gore" instead of blood that was to be shed; and there was a great deal about the "clank of the tyrant's chain," and the "blood-stained sword," and such other fuliginous figures of speech. Sometimes there was a good deal of force behind this sounding rhetoric, as in Henry Timrod's A Call to Arms and in James R. Randall's There's Life in the Old Land yet, but for the most part it had an air of bombast and turgidity, which would have given a false impression in regard to the real spirit of determination among the Southern people, if one had only judged by its inflated expression. The pages of the Southern Amaranth, and other collections of rebel poetry, give the impression of having been written by school-boys, and contain little but sophomoric rhetoric of the most sounding and inflated description. That it had a fiery energy and an invincible determination behind it was abundantly shown, but the voice of the South in its polite literature was one of inflated extravagance. Nevertheless it produced the most manly and vigorous song of the whole war in Dr. J. W. Palmer's Stonewall Jackson's Way; and some verses appeared in a Richmond paper in 1861, entitled Call All, which have a fiery energy and directness unsurpassed, and were in the genuine language of the people: —

CALL ALL.

Whoop! the Doodles have broken loose,
Roaring around like the very deuce.
Lice of Egypt, a hungry pack;
After 'em, boys, and drive 'em back,

Bull-dog, terrier, cur, and fice,
Back to the beggarly land of ice.
Worry 'em, bite 'em, scratch and tear
Everybody and everywhere.

Old Kentucky is caved from under;
Tennessee is split asunder,
Alabama awaits attack,
And Georgia bristles up her back.

Old John Brown is dead and gone,
Still his spirit is marching on, —
Lantern-jawed, and legs, my boys,
Long as an ape's from Illinois.

Want a weapon? Gather a brick,
A club or cudgel, a stone or stick,
Anything with a blade or butt,
Anything that can cleave or cut;

Anything heavy, or hard, or keen;
Any sort of slaying machine;
Anything with a willing mind
And the steady arm of a man behind.

Want a weapon? Why, capture one;
Every Doodle has got a gun,

Belt and bayonet, bright and new.
Kill a Doodle and capture two!

Shoulder to shoulder, son and sire,
All, call all! to the feast of fire,
Mother and maiden, child and slave,
A common triumph or a single grave.

The street ballad did not exist in the South, so far as I can discover, and the popular song-books were very few in comparison with those of the North. There were some, however, printed on discolored paper and with worn-out type. Among them were The New Confederate Flag Songster, S. C. Griggs, Mobile; The General Lee Songster, John C. Schreiner & Son, Macon and Savannah; The Jack Morgan Songster, compiled by a captain in General Lee's army; and Songs of Love and Liberty, compiled by a North Carolina lady, Raleigh, 1864. Like the Northern song-books, they contained an admixture of the popular negro melodies with the songs of the war, and there are but few instances of any genuine and native expression. The song which gave the title to The Jack Morgan Songster, however, has a good deal of force and vigor, and was evidently written by the camp fire. It is entitled Three Cheers for our Jack Morgan: —

The snow is in the cloud,
And night is gathering o'er us,

The winds are piping loud,
   And fan the flame before us.
Then join the jovial band,
   And tune the vocal organ,
And with a will we'll all join in
   Three cheers for our Jack Morgan.

Chorus. Gather round the camp fire,
     Our duty has been done,
   Let's gather round the camp fire
     And have a little fun.
   Let's gather round the camp fire,
     Our duty has been done,
   'Twas done upon the battle field,
     Three cheers for our Jack Morgan.

Jack Morgan is his name,
   The peerless and the lucky;
No dastard foe can tame
   The son of old Kentucky.
His heart is with his State,
   He fights for Southern freedom;
His men their General's word await,
   They'll follow where he'll lead 'em.

He swore to free his home,
   To burst her chains asunder,
With sound of trump and drum
   And loud Confederate thunder.
And in the darksome night,
   By light of homesteads burning,
He puts the skulking foe to flight,
   Their hearts to wailings turning.

The dungeon, dark and cold,
  Could not his body prison,
Nor tame a spirit bold
  That o'er reverse had risen.
Then sing the song of joy,
  Our toast is lovely woman,
And Morgan he's the gallant boy
  To plague the hated foeman.

The tone of the Southern songs was not only a good deal more ferocious and savage than that of those of the North, but there were fewer indications of that spirit of humor which pervaded the Northern camps, and found expression in the soldiers' songs. There is, however, one Southern piece of verse, descriptive of the emotions of the newly drafted conscript, which has an original flavor of comicality, although evidently inspired by the spirit of Yankee Doodle: —

THE VALIANT CONSCRIPT.

How are you, boys? I'm just from camp,
  And feel as brave as Cæsar;
The sound of bugle, drum, and fife
  Has raised my Ebenezer.
I'm full of fight, odds shot and shell,
  I'll leap into the saddle,
And when the Yankees see me come,
  Lord, how they will skedaddle!

Hold up your head, up, Shanghai, Shanks,
  Don't shake your knees and blink so,

It is no time to dodge the act;
  Brave comrades, don't you think so?

I was a ploughboy in the field,
  A gawky, lazy dodger,
When came the conscript officer
  And took me for a sodger.
He put a musket in my hand,
  And showed me how to fire it;
I marched and countermarched all day;
  Lord, how I did admire it!

With corn and hog fat for my food,
  And digging, guarding, drilling,
I got as thin as twice-skimmed milk,
  And was scarcely worth the killing.
And now I'm used to homely fare,
  My skin as tough as leather,
I do guard duty cheerfully
  In every kind of weather.

I'm brimful of fight, my boys,
  I would not give a "thank ye"
For all the smiles the girls can give
  Until I've killed a Yankee.
High private is a glorious rank,
  There's wide room for promotion;
I'll get a corporal's stripes some day,
  When fortune's in the notion.

'T is true I have not seen a fight,
  Nor have I smelt gunpowder,

But then the way I'll pepper 'em
    Will be a sin to chowder.
A sergeant's stripes I now will sport,
    Perhaps be color-bearer,
And then a captain — good for me —
    I'll be a regular tearer.

I'll then begin to wear the stars,
    And then the wreaths of glory,
Until the army I command,
    And poets sing my story.
Our Congress will pass votes of thanks
    To him who rose from zero,
The people in a mass will shout,
    Hurrah, behold the hero!
        (*Fires his gun by accident.*)

What's that? oh dear! a boiler's burst,
    A gaspipe has exploded,
Maybe the Yankees are hard by
    With muskets ready loaded.
On, gallant soldiers, beat 'em back,
    I'll join you in the frolic,
But I've a chill from head to foot,
    And symptoms of the colic.

    The spirit of the Southern women is well known to have been as vigorous and determined as that of their brothers, and the sacrifices which they were compelled to make were much more severe and general than at the North. They had been dependent upon the North and foreign countries for clothing and the luxuries of the household, and when these sources of supply were cut off by the war and the blockade, they had to make and sew their own homespun dresses, and forego all the delights of fashion and adornment. The sacrifices and devotion of the daughters of the South were sung in turgid rhetoric, like the threats and appeals of the men, but here is a genuine voice, evidently a woman's own, which speaks for her sisters in their homelier trials, as well as in their deeper emotions: —

THE SOUTHERN GIRL'S SONG.

Oh yes, I am a Southern girl,
    And glory in the name,
And boast it with far greater pride
    Than glittering wealth or fame.
We envy not the Northern girl
    With robes of beauty rare,
Though diamonds grace her snowy neck
    And pearls bedeck her hair.

Hurrah, hurrah,
    For the sunny South so dear.
Three cheers for the homespun dress
    That Southern ladies wear!

The homespun dress is plain, I know,
    My hat's palmetto, too,
But then it shows what Southern girls
    For Southern rights will do.

We have sent the bravest of our land
　　To battle with the foe,
And we will lend a helping hand ;
　　We love the South, you know.

Now, Northern goods are out of date,
　　And since old Abe's blockade,
We Southern girls can be content
　　With goods that 's Southern made.
We sent our sweethearts to the war,
　　But, dear girls, never mind,
Your soldier love will ne'er forget
　　The girl he left behind.

The soldier is the lad for me,
　　A brave heart I adore ;
And when the sunny South is free,
　　And when the fight is no more,
I 'll choose me then a lover brave
　　From out the gallant band ;
The soldier lad I love the best
　　Shall have my heart and hand.

The Southern land 's a glorious land,
　　And has a glorious cause ;
Then cheer, three cheers for Southern rights
　　And for the Southern boys.
We 'll scorn to wear a bit of silk,
　　A bit of Northern lace ;
And make our homespun dresses up,
　　And wear them with such grace.

And now, young men, a word to you :
　　If you would win the fair,

> Go to the field where honor calls
>   And win your lady there.
> Remember that our brightest smiles
>   Are for the true and brave,
> And that our tears are all for those
>   Who fill a soldier's grave.

The folk-songs of the civil war, in which millions were engaged and which lasted for four years, do not compare in quality with those which much lighter struggles have produced, notably the Jacobite rebellion in Scotland. The Americans were not a singing people in the bent of their genius, and the conditions of life and civilization were not favorable to this form of expression. The newspaper had taken the place of the ballad as a means of influencing the public mind, and poetry had passed from the people to the literary artists. So when the great crisis of the civil war came, affecting all minds and all hearts, the people were unfamiliar with this mode of expression, and the literary artists had not the power to interpret their feelings except in their own artificial forms without touching the heart or giving vital meaning to the voice. The accident of the combination of genius with this sincerity, which produced La Marseillaise and Der Wacht am Rhein, did not occur, so that the great struggle is without an equally great song embodying and interpreting the spirit of the nation, and whatever fine poems and songs there were distinctly fall below this ideal. But in such a struggle the voice of the people could not fail to find expression by the means which the history of mankind has shown to be the most natural expression of emotion and enthusiasm, and their songs, however imperfect, either as literature or popular poetry, are the most genuine expression of the feelings and thoughts which filled their hearts and minds, and have a genuineness which informs the rude or inadequate words, and are a most important illustration of the history of that tremendous conflict.

ENGLISH AND SCOTTISH POPULAR BALLADS.

PROFESSOR FRANCIS JAMES CHILD'S edition of the English and Scottish Popular Ballads, monumental in size, is still more monumental in the labor which it represents. It embodies not only diligent research for the most authentic and original versions of the ancient ballads in all the known sources in print or in manuscript, and the recovery of many from still living traditions in Great Britain and the United States, but a careful study and comparison of the folk-song of kindred European nations and of the world for resemblances in subject and story; thus making a most interesting and valuable addition to the knowledge of the common development of the human intellect in primitive thought and form of expression in diverse countries. How much study this has involved can only be appreciated by those who have seen its results in the concise introductions to each ballad, citing comparisons in every known literature, and yet further work in this direction will be left for later scholars, as the study and collection of folk-song is being pursued with more and more zeal and success in every quarter of the world, under the appreciation of its great literary as well as historical value. Professor Child has been governed by the strictest conscientiousness in giving his version of the popular ballads, not only going to the original sources like the Percy folio, the manuscript materials for The Minstrelsy of the Scottish Border preserved at Abbotsford, Motherwell's note books, and other manuscripts and stall copies, but reprinting them with all their omissions and defects, not supplying the most obvious missing word or even letter without indicating it. He has not followed the example of the strictly faithful editors of the ancient ballads like Motherwell in presenting alone the most complete and perfect specimen, nor allowed himself like others, substantially faithful, like Scott and Jamieson, to collate a number of copies derived from different sources into a harmonious whole, but gives each version distinct in itself, even to a solitary variant verse. It is one of the commonplaces of the history of English and Scottish ballad poetry that most of its collectors and editors from Bishop Percy downward have felt themselves entitled to amend and correct the imperfect fragments to a greater or less degree, supplying missing lines or stanzas to connect or complete the story, and that this has resulted sometimes in the most incongruous patchwork in which the sentiments and poetical fashions of one generation have been foisted upon those of another to the utter destruction of all verisimilitude, to say nothing of strength and genuineness of expression. Bishop Percy, with all his fine taste and genuine poetic power, was a conspicuous sinner in this respect, and patched the rough and strong frieze of the ancient ballads with pieces of the thin and sleazy silk of eighteenth century sentiment and diction. Even Scott, with all his sense of honesty and appreciation of the value of the integrity of the ancient ballads, could not always refrain from his possessing temptation " to give a hat and stick" to the stories which he heard, and, as Professor Child points out, there are some stanzas in the Border Minstrelsy which bear suspiciously his mark, and of which the originals have not been found in his manuscript materials. It is true enough that Scott's additions and emendations, as well as those of Allan Cunningham, who was wholly indifferent to the genuineness and integrity of his originals, were likely to be in the very spirit and turn of expression of the ancient ballads, and that the lover of poetry for its own sake will not be likely to find fault with them, but the real student of folk-song must repudiate them, and can be content only with the genuine expressions of the people, as they lived in tradition, however inchoate and imperfect they may be. The historical and ethnological value of the ancient ballads consists in their absolute genuineness, and even the imperfection of their utterances illustrates the condition of the popular mind and the characteristics of the individual intelligence which produced them, and are important geological evidences of the growth and development of the human intellect. At the same time this very imperfection of speech, and the struggle of primitive thought to express itself in language sometimes creates, as it were by accident, the very flower of strength and vividness in picturesque description, and the interpretation of emotion as the most skillful art has been unable to do. How strong these ballads were, and what a hold they had upon the minds and imaginations of the people, as the interpretation of their innate poetic spirit, is shown in the tenacity with which they have lived, and been reproduced in varying forms through generations down to the present day. Ballads like The Cruel Sister and Lord Thomas and Fair Annet, the production probably of the sixteenth or seventeenth century, have been recovered, with the essential burden of their verse and the subject of their story, from the mouths of English peasants and Irish servant girls, and in the folk-lore of the American nursery, to which they had been transmitted simply by the force of oral tradition, and without any assistance from print; and it is not likely that they will entirely disappear for generations to come, any more than the perennial nursery tales which were created by and appeal to the primitive and childish imagination. These traditional versions have been altered to suit the localities, and weakened in their coherence and vigor of expression from the time when they were the literature of the main body of the people instead of the lowest class, as the stall copies of the ballads of the ancient minstrels, when they were the attendants of kings and nobles and shared the inspiration of chivalry, have been degraded to the level of the intelligence of the audience of the street singers or the gatherings in the taprooms of the village alehouses; but they retain the essential characteristics of simple emotion, inherent melody, and primitive language, and have still something of the fine and penetrating flavor of popular romance.

It is almost needless to say to the student of literature that the art of popular ballad writing is extinct, or is successful only in the rarest instances. Poets of genuine power and inspiration, imbued and saturated with the spirit of the ancient ballads, have attempted to re-create them in the telling of an ancient or modern story, but, whatever their original power or imitative skill, they have failed to reproduce that native strength and peculiar flavor of expression which gives the ancient ballads such a hold upon the mind. The modern ballads are admired by the intellect rather than felt by the heart, and are recognized as the product of skillful art rather than as the expression of original emotion. Even Scott, whose literary genius was so saturated with their spirit, and Wordsworth, who sought his inspiration in the simple emotions of the peasant heart and interpreted them so perfectly in a literary form of glowing simplicity, could not produce a popular ballad, and even Coleridge's Ancient Mariner, with all its powerful and naked mystery and natural archaism of thought and language, appeals to the literary rather than to the popular imagination. All the more absolute imitations of ancient literature, like those of Rossetti and Morris, have still more the air of unreality, in spite of what is oftentimes their very great power and skill, and Sir Samuel Ferguson's Lays of the Western Gael, perfect as they are in the reproduction of the Celtic spirit and expression, are for the admiration of scholars rather than the feeling of the people. It is hardly too much to say that in modern English literature there are but two poems which fulfill the conditions of the ancient ballads in their simplicity, directness, and originality of language, their power upon the mind and heart through the ear, and the indefinable flavor of primitive emotion, and those very different in style, subject, and form of expression. These are Cowper's Loss of the Royal George, and Rudyard Kipling's Danny Deever. Every one who has heard it or read it can repeat, —

> Toll for the brave,
> The brave that are no more,
> Sunk beneath the wave
> Fast by their native shore ;

and the burden and the measure, the simplicity and strength of diction, of Danny Deever are equally calculated to take a possessing hold upon the ear. These ballads are not imitations derived from study of the ancient popular ballads, but obtaining their inspiration from the same original source in strong and primitive emotion interpreted in the simplest language possible, and speaking through the ear by the chanted rather than through the eye by the printed line. It is this appeal to the ear which is the strongest characteristic of the form of the ancient ballads. They were made to be sung or chanted rather than read, and therefore they have a felicity of sound as an interpreter of meaning which is often perfect in its expression ; and when imperfect, that is, when the meaning is not clear, but is only vaguely and dimly attached to the sound, as in the refrains and burdens, there is a flavor or an atmosphere of meaning which pervades it and adds to the effect.

There is a touch of the plaintiveness of natural sounds which no literary art could give in the opening of The Queen of Elphan's Nourrice: —

> I heard a cow low, a bonnie cow low,
>   An' a cow low down in yon fauld.
> Long, long will my young son greet
>   Or his mother take him from cauld.

Even when the burden is still more arbitrary, and without any direct reflection of the meaning whatever, it is never felt to be incongruous or artificial, and has a mystic and intensifying effect, as in the painful ballad of The Sheath and Knife: —

> He has made a grave that was long and deep,
>   The broom blooms bonnie, and says it is fair,
> And he's buried his sister, with her babe at her feet,
>   And they'll never gang down to the broom any mair.

And even when the refrain might be called simply a meaningless chant, it makes a part of the ballad which could not be taken away without a loss of the quality which gives it a living voice, as in the chorus, which sings of itself to The Elfin Knight:

> My plaid awa, my plaid awa,
>   And o'er the hills and far awa,
>   And far awa to Norowa.
> My plaid shall not be blawn awa.

As to these stanzas and lines, which give a perfect marriage of sound and meaning either in the interpretation of emotion or description, and in which the ear is the interpreter of the eye and the heart with a skill which no art could give, they are numberless, and of the very substance of the genius of the old ballad singers. There is nothing in the cultivated skill of trochee and spondee to equal such untaught perfections of the human voice as these: —

> O, we were sisters, sisters seven;
> We were the fairest under heaven.
> (Gil Brenton.)

> And a lightsome bugle then heard he blowe,
> Over the bents sae browne.
> (Sir Cawline.)

> It was a sad and rainy night,
> As ever rained from town to town.
> (Clerk Saunders.)

> But 't was wind and weet and fire and sleet
> When we came to the castle wa.
> (Kinmont Willie.)

> O, he has ridden o'er field and fell
> Through ruins and moss and many a mire,
> He spurs a steed that was sair to ride,
> And frae her forefeet flew the fire.
> (Annan Water.)

And this, in which the very gallop of the horse's feet runs along the lines: —

> It's twenty lang miles to Sillerton toun,
>   The langest that ever were gane,
> But the steed it was wight and the lady was light,
>   And she rade linkin in.
>
> (Prince Robert.)

The element of poetry of the highest kind in these ballads is the strength as well as the simplicity of passion interpreted in language of naked directness and dramatic power. Their stories are mainly those of the bloody tragedies and the violent events and emotions in the lives of a people to whom strife and adventure were an integral part of existence, and whose passions were strong and vigorous, although a proportion of the ballads have an element of rustic humor, and the cycle of those relating to Robin Hood is mainly of this kind. There is an element of the supernatural in the English and Scottish ballads, more particularly in the latter, which, if not so marked and pervading as in those of the Celtic nations, shows that the mysterious terrors of nature were still embodied in the visible forms of the imagination, and that the woods were still haunted by elfin knights, the green braes by fairies, while human beings were still liable to be transformed into laidly worms and foul toads by the enchantment of witches, in at least a pervading shadow of popular belief. But for the most part they were singularly free from the tincture of the marvelous, and mainly the simple chronicles of stirring events or the tragedies of passion. This gives them an element of strength, which is wanting to the phantasmagorial figures of more imaginative nations, whatever glow of misty glory shines about them as in the creations of the early Celtic bards. The impression of the soul of nature is strong but not overpowering as in these latter, and the influence of the landscape and the sky in storm or calm illuminates but does not interfere with the dramatic action. As has been said, strength of thought and strength of language are their prevailing characteristics. Their strength of language is that which belongs to the speech of a people when it is fresh and new, and before it has been overlaid with words created for literary purposes and by the introduction of foreign words to give niceties of meaning, and no cultivated language has the same power and directness as that which is the simple expression of the thoughts of the people. Goethe, with his sound critical insight, noted this when he said, "The unsophisticated man is the more master of direct, effective expression than he who has had a regular training," and a language may often lose in strength what it gains in ornament and flexibility. This strength of expression is written large over all the English and Scottish ballads, and specimens are merely arbitrary and may be taken almost at random:—

>Aye she waukened at the dead man,
> And aye she waukened him to and fro.
>   (Clerk Saunders.)

>And when she came out of the Kirk,
> She shimmered like the sun.
>   (Lord Thomas and Fair Annet.)

>The Lindsays flew like fire about,
> Till all the fray was done.
>   (The Battle of Otterbourne.)

>One spak slow, and another whispered out,
> She 's gone wi' Gipsy Davy.
>   (The Gipsy Laddy.)

>Twice it lifted its bonnie blue ee,
>Thae looks gae through the saul o' me.
>   (The Cruel Mother.)

>There was no maen made for that lady,
> In bower where she lay dead,
>But a' was for the bonnie babe,
> That lay blabbering in her bleed.
>   (Lord Ingram and Child Wyett.)

>O, then she stood and better she stood,
> And never did shed a tear,

Till once she saw her seven brethren slain,
    And her father she loved sae dear.
(The Douglas Tragedy.)

And when he came to her bower she was pale and wan,
But she grew red and ruddy, when Glenlogie came in.
(Glenlogie.)

The dramatic power of expression, that which illumines it with a touch of action, is not less remarkable than that of direct phraseology: —

"Hold up, hold up, Lord William," she says,
    "I fear that you are slain."
"It's nothing but the shadow of my scarlet cloak,
    That shines in the water sae plain."
(Earl Brand.)

And aye she served the lang table,
    With white bread and with brown,
And aye she turned her round about,
    Sae fast the tears fell down.
(Fair Annie.)

She turned her head on her left shoulder,
    Saw her girdle hang on a tree,
O, God bless those that gave me that,
    They'll never give more to me.
(Lary Maissy.)

When I rose up in the morn,
    My goodly palace for to lea,

> I knocked at my lord's chamber door,
>   But never a word wad he speak to me.
>   (Jamie Douglass.)

> The King looked over his left shoulder,
>   And a grim look looked he,
> Earl Martial an' 't were na for my oath
>   Or hanged thou shouldst be.
>   (Queen Elinor's Confession.)

The look cast over the shoulder is a very familiar action in the ballads, as is also that where an angry man strikes the table with his hand and "keps" it with his knee. Every one who receives the letter is described as first smiling and then having his eyes filled with tears, as in Sir Patrick Spence, and almost in an exact repetition of the language, and there are numerous actions and phases which are the common stock of the ballad poets. The idea of the exclusive rights to poetical property and of the sin of plagiarism does not seem to have occurred to them, and they took a striking image or an effective phrase wherever they found it as a part of the common stock of poetry. These familiar and striking phrases doubtless added to the effect, being recognized as old friends by the audience, and, like the repetitions of words and action by a number of persons in the same ballad, such as by the members of a family in succession denying the prayer of an unfortunate, emphasizing and deepening the impression. Certain adjectives also became attached to words as a part of their property, such as red to gold and wan to water, and are essential parts of the ballad language, which add to its effect by constant repetition.

One of the charms of these ancient ballads is the appreciation of the effects of nature, given sometimes with a magical effect of suddenness and originality. What can be more effective, for instance, than the touch of beauty and charm in the tragedy of Babylon : —

> He 's killed the maid and he 's laid her by
> To bear the red rose company.

And can we not feel the magic of the note of elfin horn, touching the heart with irresistible call through the summer air, in the opening to Hind Etin ? —

> Lady Margaret sits at her bower door,
>   Sewing her silken seam ;
> She heard a note in Elmond wood,
>   And wished she there had been.

The voice of the unseen sea gives a note of deep solemnity and terror to the supernatural landscape through which Thomas, the Rhymer, journeys with the elfin queen : —

And they rode on and farther on,
   And they waded the river above the knee,
And they saw neither sun nor moon,
   But they heard the roaring of the sea.

How the strength of a lover's thought is illuminated by the touch of nature itself in **Willie and Alison**: —

When he was in his saddle set,
   And slowly ridin' on his way,
He had more mind o' Alison
   Than he had o' the light o' day.

These touches of the power of nature upon human action, and revealing human thought, are scattered throughout the ballads, and have the effect of perfect naturalness and simplicity, as though the heart and not the mind spoke in them.

A specimen of the ancient ballad in its most perfect strength, absolute and concise in its construction, without wandering into irrelevancies and incongruities, as many of them do, and in which the appalling tragedy strikes with a sudden blow upon the heart at its close, is **Edward**. It has all the characteristic features of the ballads, in the vivid colors of nature illuminating and intensifying his dramatic dialogue, while it has the mist of blood in the witchlike questions of its opening, and the passion of hatred and despair in its close.

Ballads of similar form and subject are to be found in Scandinavian literature, and counterparts to its methods of revelation in various English and Scottish ballads, but none have so pure a construction and so perfect an effect as this: —

"Why does your brand sae drap wi' bluid,
    Edward, Edward?
Why does your brand sae drap wi' bluid,
    And why sae sad gang yee, O?"
"O, I hae killed my hauke sae guid,
    Mither, mither.
O, I hae killed my hauke sae guid,
    And I had nae mair but hee, O."

"Your hauke's bluid was nevir sae reid,
    Edward, Edward.
Your hauke's bluid was nevir sae reid,
    My deir son, I tell thee, O."
'O, I hae killed my red roan steed,
    Mither, mither.
O, I hae killed my red roan steed
    That was sae fair and free, O."

"Your steed was auld and ye hae gat mair,
    Edward, Edward.
Your steed was auld and ye hae got mair.
    Sum other dule ye drie, O."
"O, I hae killed my fadir deir,
    Mither, mither.
O, I hae killed my fadir deir.
    Alas! and wae is mee, O."

"And whatten penance will ye drie for that,
  Edward, Edward?
And whatten penance will ye drie for that,
  My deir son? Now tell mee, O."
"I 'll set my feit in yonder boat,
  Mither, mither.
I 'll set my feit in yonder boat,
  And I 'll fare ovir the sea, O."

"And what will you doe wi' your towirs and your ha',
  Edward, Edward?
And what will you doe wi' your towirs and your ha',
  That were sae fair and free, O?"
"I 'll let them stand tul they down fa',
  Mither, mither.
I 'll let them stand tul they down fa',
  For here nevir mair maun I bee, O."

"And what wul ye leave to your bairns and your wife,
  Edward, Edward?
And what wul ye leave to your bairns and your wife,
  When ye gang ovir the sea, O?"
"The warlde's room, late them beg thrae life,
  Mither, mither.
The warlde's room, late them bag thrae life,
  For them nevir mair wul I see, O."

"And what wul ye leave to your ain mither, deir,
  Edward, Edward?
And what wul ye leave to your ain mither, deir,
  My deir son? Now tell mee, O."
"The curse of hell frae me sall ye beir,
  Mither, mither.

> The curse of hell frae me sall ye beir,
>   Sic counseils ye gave to me, O."

Edward was communicated to Bishop Percy from Scotland by Lord Hailes, and there is some affectation in the ancient spelling, but it is undoubtedly genuine, and, as Professor Child remarks, " as spelling will not make an old ballad, so it will not unmake one."

One of the most famous and best known of the ancient Scottish ballads is that entitled Waly, Waly, gin Love be Bony, or, as it is sometimes called, Lady Anne Bothwell's Lament, which was first published in Ramsay's Tea Table Miscellany. It has numerous variants embodying the language of the lament in stories of a more dramatic character, founded on a tradition of the Douglas family, but this has the strength and simplicity of an original:—

> O, waly, waly, up the bank,
>   And waly, waly, down the brae;
> And waly, waly, yon burn-side,
>   Where I and my love wont to gae.
>
> I leaned my back unto an aik,
>   I thought it was a trusty tree;
> But first it bowed, and syne it brak,
>   Sae my true love did lightly me.
>
> O, waly, waly, but love be bony,
>   A little time, while it is new;

But when it's auld it waxeth cauld,
   And fades away like morning dew.

O, wherefore should I brush my head?
   O, wherefore should I kaim my hair,
For my true love has me forsook,
   And says he'll never love me mair.

Now, Arthur's seat shall be my bed,
   The sheets shall ne'er be fyld by me;
Saint Anton's well shall be my drink
   Since my true love's forsaken me.

Martinmas wind, when wilt thou blow,
   And shake the green leaves off the tree?
O, gentle death, when wilt thou come,
   For of my life I am weary.

'T is not the frost that freezes fell,
   Nor blawing snaw's inclemency;
'T is not the cauld as makes me cry,
   But my love's heart grown cauld to me.

When we came in by Glasgow town,
   We were a comelie sight to see;
My love was clad in black velvet,
   And I myself in cramoisie.

But had I wist before I kist
   That love had been sae ill to win;
I'd locked my heart in a case of gold,
   And pinned it with a silver pin.

> Oh, oh, if my young babe was born,
> And set upon the nurse's knee;
> And I mysell were dead and gone,
> For a maid again I'll never be.

The burden of this lament, its simple passion appealing to the popular heart and its melody holding the ear, has been perpetuated through the generations since it was first sung. It has been printed in all forms and variations in the broadsides and penny song books, as well as in the critical collections of poetry, solaced the sentimental feeling of the dairy maid as well as haunted the vision of Charles Lamb, and its refrain may be heard to-day in the burlesque choruses of the negro minstrel stage. A very interesting example is given by Professor Child of the way in which an old ballad of perfect form and construction may be made incoherent and shapeless in a broadside copy, mere matter of "silly sooth" for old age or primitive ignorance, without losing the fine flower of pathos and feeling, or the grace of expression, in its disconnected and ejaculatory stanzas. It is also interesting as an example, of which many others could be given, of the effect of oral tradition passing from minds of native strength, if without education, down to and through those of a lower order of intelligence, from whom now only the débris of the ancient songs and ballads can be obtained.

It is from a broadside printed in Edinburgh, without date, but of considerable antiquity, and entitled Arthur's Seat shall be My Bed, etc., or Love in Despair.

> Come lay me soft and draw me near,
>   And lay thy white hand over me;
> For I am starving in the cold,
>   And thou art bound to cover me.
>
> O, cover me in my distress,
>   And help me in my miserie;
> For I do wake, when I should sleep,
>   All for the love of my dearie.
>
> My rents they are but very small,
>   For to maintain my love withall;
> But with my labour and my pain,
>   I will maintain my love with them.
>
> O, Arthur's seat shall be my bed,
>   And the sheets shall never be filed by me,
> St. Anthony's well shall be my drink,
>   Since my true love's forsaken me.
>
> Should I be bound, that may go free?
> Should I love them that love not me?
> I'll rather travel into Spain,
>   Where I'll get love for love again.
>
> And I'll cast off my robes of black,
>   And will put on the robes of blue;

And I will come to some other land
　To see if my love will on me rue.

It is not the cold that makes me cry,
It is not the weet that wearies me ;
Nor is it the frost that freezes fell,
But I love a lad, and I dare not tell.

Oh, faith is gone, and truth is past,
　And my true love's forsaken me ;
If all be true that I hear say,
　I'll mourn until the day I die.

Oh, if I had nere been born,
　That to have died, when I was young ;
Then I had never wet my cheeks
　For the love of any woman's son.

Oh, oh, if my young babe was born,
　And set upon the nurse's knee ;
And I myself were dead and gone,
　For a maid again I shall never be.

Martinmas wind, when wilt thou blow,
　And blow the green leefs off the tree ;
O gentle Death, when wilt thou come,
　For of my life I am wearie.

As in all single hearts and primitive natures, the visible features of death, the white shroud and the grave, "hap'd with the sods sae green," make a deep impression, and the imagination concerning the loved one lost is not lifted to spiritual forms, but dwells upon the painful figures of the charnel house. The ghosts that visit the living have the fatal breath of decaying mortality, and are summoned back by the cock to the winding sheet and the worm. The ballads that deal with this subject are all in the same strain, and repeat the same phrases. The lady asks her dead lover if there is any room at his head or any room at his feet in his new bed, and he answers that there is none, it is made so narrow, and that the worms are his only bedfellows; and warns her that he cannot give the kiss she craves, for his breath would be fatal. Sometimes the images of mortality are extremely powerful as well as grotesque, as in the ballad of Sweet William's Ghost: —

> My meikle toe is my gavil post,
> My nose is my roof tree,
> My ribs are kebars to my house;
> There is no room for thee.

Sometimes they have a touch of homely pathos, which relieves them from the conventional note of sorrow, as when the three sons of The Wife of Usher's Well are called back to the grave by the crowing cock, and the youngest says: —

> Fare ye weel, my mother, dear;
> Farewell to barn and byre,

And fare ye weel, the bonny lass,
That kindles my mother's fire.

One of the most interesting specimens of the ballads of this kind, as they exist to-day, borrowed in a modified form from the ancient, but embodying a still popular superstition, is The Unquiet Grave, recently taken down from the lips of a young girl in Sussex. It is founded on the belief, common to many primitive peoples, that excessive weeping disturbs the repose of the departed, and has a touch of that natural originality of description and that abruptness which presupposes a quickness of appreciation, which does not require an elaborate story to make the connection intelligible, characteristic of popular poetry, and which shows that the elements of mind to which it is addressed are always the same: —

> The wind doth blow to-day, my love,
>   And a few small drops of rain.
> I never had but one true love —
>   In the cold grave she was lain.
>
> I'll do as much for my true love
>   As any young man may,
> I'll sit and mourn all at her grave
>   For a twelvemonth and a day.
>
> The twelvemonth and a day being up,
>   The dead began to speak:

"O, who sits weeping on my grave
    And will not let me sleep?"

"'T is I, my love, sits on your grave
    And will not let you sleep;
For I crave one kiss of your clay-cold lips,
    And that is all I seek."

"You crave one kiss of my clay-cold lips,
    But your breath smells earthly strong;
If you have one kiss of my clay-cold lips
    Your time will not be long."

'T is down in yonder garden green,
    Love, where we used to walk:
The finest flower that e'er was seen
    Is withered on the stalk.

The stalk is withered dry, my love,
    So will our hearts decay:
So make yourself content, my love,
    Till God calls you away.

By far the larger number of the popular ballads had their origin in Scotland, and they are also of much finer quality than those of England. Even if the question of the origin of the ballad of Chevy Chace should be decided in favor of the latter, it would simply be localized upon the Border within the limit of Scottish influence. The English ballads are mostly heavy and dull, imperfect in form and expression, in comparison with the Scottish, and show few signs of the depth and glow of feeling in the burning words of the latter. The English ballads relating to King Arthur are greatly inferior in strength and spirit to the prose chronicles, and their dealing with the marvelous is coarse and commonplace in comparison with the spiritual and majestic mystery of the Welsh cycle of Arthurian romance. And the English ballads continued to degenerate, rather than improve, from the rude vigor of some of the Arthurian ballads, and took on the element of coarse humor which is characteristic of the Robin Hood cycle, from which nearly every gleam of poetry is eliminated. It may be said that the degeneracy of the English popular ballad was due to the spread of education among the people, and the development of their genius in more strictly literary forms under the influence of Chaucer and his associates. But the spread of education and the increase of literary production among the English people was by no means so general as to affect the quality of the popular ballad at this period, and certainly less than that which prevailed in Scotland at a later time, when the production of popular poetry was in its fullest flower. The adventures of the English outlaws, of whom Robin Hood, however mythical his actual existence, was the type, were not less stirring and full of the natural elements of poetry than those of the reivers and cattle thieves of the Scottish Border, but the ballads of the former cycle are only full of a vulgar peasant humor, while the latter are illuminated with the light of battle, and have the quarter staff and broken pate in place of the spear and the bleeding breast. Of Robin Hood it is said: —

> Then Robin took them both by the hand,
> And danced about the oke tree;
> For three merry men and three merry men
> And three merry men are we.

While the Lord of Branxholm cries:

> Gae warn the water broad and wide,
> Gae warn it sune and hastilie;
> He that winna ride for Telfer's Kyle
> Let him neer look in the face o' me.

and the difference in the spirit is reflected in the quality of the verse, the one dull and commonplace, suited to an audience of heavy-faced rustics in an alehouse, and the other full of fire and vigor, fit to be chanted in the dining hall of a Border chief. It is impossible to analyze ethnologically the causes of the great superiority of the Scottish popular poetry, or to define how much of the elevation of feeling and appreciation of the magic of nature came from the greater admixture of the Celtic element, which in its turn was given force and vigor, directness of expression and coherence of construction by the stronger nature of the invading element, which, for the want of a more definite term, is called Saxon. The effect of these influences is merely conjectural, as is also that of the country itself, its natural scenery, the disturbed life of the people, and the ferment of the popular mind. It can only be said that there was something in the national genius of the Lowland Scotch different from that of their more stolid neighbors at the south and their more mystical neighbors at the north, and which fitted them for the production of popular poetry in song and ballad at once elevated and impassioned, and which has resulted in a quantity and quality which no other province of the world has rivaled. It is known over the world, and has been translated into almost every literary language of Europe. To the English reader it is only necessary to give the titles to recall the verses that cling to the memory, and express the deepest glow of passion and pathos in words whose magic melody is beyond the reach of art, and which are winged with a force above the powers of uninspired speech. The Border Widow tells how she buried her slain husband: —

> I took his body on my back,
> And whiles I gaed and whiles I sat,

I digged a grave and laid him in,
    And happd him with sod sae green.

Lord Randal comes home to his mother from his false love's poisoned banquet: —

O, where hae ye been, Lord Randal, my son,
    O, where hae ye been, my handsome young man;
I have been to the greenwood; mither, mak my bed soon,
    For I 'm wearie wi hunting and fain wald lie down."

The lady of the House of Airlie cries out from the burning reek to the cruel Edom o' Gordon: —

"Were my good lord but here this day,
    As he 's awa wi Charlie;
The dearest blood o' a' thy men
    Wad sloken the lowe o' Airlie."

Johnnie Armstrong gives his last "Good Night" in defiance: —

O, how John looked over his left shoulder,
    And to his merry men thus spoke he;
"I have asked grace of a graceless face,
    No pardon here for you and me."

Mary Hamilton cries from the gallows-tree in a burst of anguish: —

O, little did my mother ken,
    The day she cradled me,
The land I was to travel in,
    The death I was to dee.

These verses, and many like them, cling to the tongues and have sunk deep into the hearts of men, and will live until the speech in which they were created has passed away. The Flower of Yarrow will always utter her melodious lament so long as there is English poetry, and the Border moss-troopers will ride with spear in hand and "splent on spauld" until the valleys of the Tweed and the Tyne are inhabited by an alien race, and the songs in which they are sung have perished like those of the Assyrian shepherds.

The collection and study of folk-song is being pursued with a vigor and a scholarly diligence which promises to leave no corner of the world unransacked, and no people, however simple and savage, neglected, and very valuable treasures of poetry have been and are being collected, which speak to the heart with the native eloquence of unsophisticated feeling and thought, and which give a more accurate knowledge of national temperament and of the stages of the development of the human intellect than any material remains or any historical records. But none have as yet been discovered, or are likely to be, which have a stronger power of original poetry, passion, and pathos, or which reveal a more vigorous and noble native genius than the ballads and songs which were produced within the limits of the little province between the Grampians and the Border.

LADY NAIRNE AND HER SONGS.

The supreme felicity of lyric song is extremely rare even in the greatest masters of the art, and seems to come from something outside of themselves, some accident of the moment, some almost fortuitous intermingling of sound with meaning, which could have been attained by no ordinary inspiration and no deliberate skill, however accomplished and sure and strong the poetical organ which produced it. It is this supreme felicity, when it occurs, by which the lyric song of man, with only the elements of harsh and prosaic speech and common words to frame it, rivals the magic of the bird's note in joyous ecstasy or sorrow, and floods the heart, as it captivates the ear, with emotions sweeter and deeper, more ethereal and more mysterious, than life had seemed able to give. It is well known that singers, whose skill in the use of their vocal organs is the result of highly trained art, giving certainty and assurance to a great natural gift, and able at all times to command what seems the full extent of their power, sometimes have moments when they surpass themselves and exceed the limits of any art, when the voice touches a note of magic melody, which they can reach by no conscious effort even in the highest moments of inspiration, and which seems to come from some power not at their conscious command. It seems to be the same in lyric poetry, and when the power does come, then we have the touch which makes it song, as the thrill of the lark, and the ecstasy of the mocking-bird in the tropic night, are songs. The magic may not be prolonged through an entire lyric. It seldom is. It may be only in a single line or in a single verse. It may not be even the highest strain of feeling or nobility of sentiment, and may even carry with it little definite meaning upon analysis. It derives its power from the magic melody as much as from the feeling or the intelligible sense of the words, and its effect is indefinable by any law of the understanding. In its highest estate it combines the most penetrating feeling with not only perfect but magic melody, but it sometimes comes in a wild refrain, in which the meaning merely floats in the words, and the rhythm, the accent, the song itself, so to speak, is predominant. For the first instance there is the perfect example of Burns, the rapture caught once for a single strain in a song, which does not rise above the level of his accomplished skill otherwise, and which has the keenest and most penetrating feeling, joined to, and permeated by, the perfect and magic melody:—

> Had we never loved sae blindly,
> Had we never loved sae kindly,
> Never met and never parted,
> We had ne'er been broken-hearted.[1]

For the second instance, where the melody is predominant over the meaning, and where the poet seemed only to be affected by the desire to frame words that would sing themselves and merely symbolize his thought, there are very many examples in the peasant poetry and folk-song of Scotland, — refrains that have no direct connection with the song, but, like the note of a second flute in a concerto, intensify the effect of the first strain by a kindred, yet diverse accentuation, as

> The broom blooms bonnie and says it is fair;

and as the most perfect specimen that occurs, the refrain to the ballad of Lord Barnard in Jamieson's collection:—

> O, wow for day!
> And dear gin it were day!
> Gin it were day and I were away,
> For I haena long time to stay.

It is only the uneducated poets who have the courage to use language arbitrarily with a purpose

---

[1] It is needless to say that the supreme felicity of these lines has been pointed out by other and more distinguished critics.

more for melody than for meaning, and when an attempt is made to reproduce its effect deliberately, as has been done by Dante Gabriel Rossetti and William Morris, the result is simply artificial and bizarre, in spite of the skill, the intensity, and the poetical power of Sister Helen, and the melody of the most perfect example of the modern imitation of the refrain in Morris's The Wind.

> Wind, Wind, thou art sad, art thou kind?
> Wind, Wind, unhappy; thou art blind,
> Yet still thou wanderest the lily seed to find.

Perhaps the most perfect example of the lyric song, in which the melody is mingled with and sustains and elevates the feeling, and both are conjoined in an effect which melts the heart and possesses the ear, although the strain is not of so high a rapture of love or sorrow as parts of Burns's Ae Fond Kiss or Lady Anne Bothwell's Balow, and is of a peaceful sweetness and resignation rather than passion, is The Land of the Leal, by Carolina, Lady Nairne. In its original and simplest form, before she had interpolated a verse to express some of her theological ideas, it is the perfect interpretation of a sweet, solemn, and simple thought, the tenderest and purest emotion, breathed in an equally simple, but absolutely perfect melody, that is like the flowing of limpid water, crystal clear and unbroken to the end. The heart of the world has responded, and it has a place like none other in the tongue of song.

> I'm wearin' awa, John,
> Like snaw-wreaths in thaw, John,
> I'm wearin awa'
>   To the land o' the leal.
>
> There's nae sorrow there, John,
> There's neither cauld nor care, John,
> The day is aye fair
>   In the land o' the leal.
>
> Our bonnie bairn's there, John,
> She was baith gude and fair, John,
> And, oh, we grudged her sair
>   To the land o' the leal.
>
> But sorrow's sel' wears past, John,
> And joy's a-comin' fast, John,
> The joy that's aye to last,
>   In the land o' the leal.
>
> Oh, dry your glist'ning ee, John,
> My saul langs to be free, John,
> And angels beckon me
>   To the land o' the leal.
>
> O, haud ye leal and true, John,
> Your day it's wearin' through, John,
> And I'll welcome you
>   To the land o' the leal.

> Now fare-ye-weel, my ain John,
> The world's cares are vain, John,
> We'll meet and will be fain
> In the land o' the leal.

The fame of the authoress, so far as she can be said to have any of her own individual personality, rests upon this song, and sufficiently, while the English language shall last, but it was not the solitary example of her genius, and her poetical work, although not great in bulk, contains other lyrics of a very high quality, with a wide range from high martial spirit and homely pathos to gay and frolicsome humor, and instinct with the vital and living element of song. Lady Nairne was almost morbidly anxious to retain her incognito as a writer during her life, so that her own husband and nearest relatives were not in the secret, and those who surmised or guessed it hardly dared to allude to it in her presence, and the veil has rested over her personality to a great degree in comparison with the flood of light poured over the words and actions of her great contemporaries, Scott and Burns, and many lesser figures in Scotch provincial literature like Professor Wilson and Hogg. Nevertheless, since her death at a very advanced age in 1846, her songs have been collected and published under her own name, and enough has been made known concerning her life and character to give to her poetry an individuality, and reveal a very gracious, noble and engaging figure.

Carolina Oliphant was born in "the auld house of Gask," in Perthshire, on the 16th of August, 1766, six years later than Robert Burns. She came of stanch Jacobite stock on both sides, her father, Laurence Oliphant, a name since made familiar by the singular and notable career of the accomplished writer, traveler, and scholar, who puzzled the world not less by his naïve religious aberrations than by his accomplishments, took up arms for the Stuarts in "the Forty-five," and suffered attainder and temporary banishment in company with his father, who had also been "out" in the Earl of Mar's rebellion in "the Fifteen." Young Laurence Oliphant, while in exile at Versailles, married his cousin, Margaret Robertson, daughter of Duncan Robertson of Strowan, chief of the clan Dorrochy. The Robertsons had also been ardent Jacobites, and suffered in purse and person for their loyalty. The grandfather, Duncan Robertson, was notable in character and personality as well in adventure and misfortune, and had his portrait painted in immortal colors by Scott as the Baron of Bradwardine. Carolina, baptized after the exiled prince, spent her infancy and early childhood on the Continent in France and Belgium, under the care of her grandmother, her parents being in feeble health, and then returned with them to the old home at Gask, where she spent her happy, healthy, and gay youth and young womanhood. From a feeble and delicate child she had grown into a strong, vigorous, and beautiful young woman, the beauty of the country-side, called "the Flower of Strathearn" and "the lovely Car," and her life was of a kind to strengthen her ardent patriotism and cultivate her fondness for the native music, poetry, and song of which Scotland was full, but whose transcendent merits were unknown and unappreciated by the literary world until they were illuminated by the light of the genius of Burns a few years later. The anecdotes of her life give a very charming picture of innocent gayety, family affection, and friendship. She played the Jacobite airs for her aged grandfather, as she afterward wrote Jacobite songs for his pleasure, and with a skill and feeling which won the difficult approval of the famous Neil Gow, the wandering fiddler, whose skill on his instrument was like that of Scott's "Wandering Willie," and whose presence at a laird's house would draw all the young people for miles around to dance to the winged notes of his strathspeys and hornpipes. She was foremost in all scenes of gayety, and is said to have taken a carriage at midnight and driven several miles to bring one of her young lady friends out of bed for a party where partners were scarce. In the simple social pleasures of the local aristocracy, the county balls and meetings, and the gatherings of the tenantry, "the Flower of Strathearn" was a conspicuous figure, while her keen eyes were taking in the queer figures that appeared later in all the glow of bright humor in The Laird of Cockpen, The County Meeting, and Jamie, the Laird. Her first verses, The Ploughman, were written for a harvest home dinner, and were read by her brother as a contribution by an unknown author. About this time the first poems of Burns made their appearance, and stirred the heart of Scotland not less by their original genius than by the revivification of the old airs and scraps of songs, finished and cleansed of their coarseness, and made to speak to the hearts of the people in the drawing-room as well as in the peasant's cottage and the taproom of the country alehouse. It was the first acknowledgment, if not the beginning, of that appreciation of the wealth of pathos and humor in the peasant poetry of Scotland, among the cultivated classes, and drew that attention and emulation to which all there is of value in modern Scotch poetry is due. It was the inspiration of the genius of Carolina Oliphant, and from this time she began to write the new verses to the old airs, and to replace the imperfect, unworthy, and sometimes coarse and vulgar scraps of songs with the beautiful ones of her own, equally Scotch and racy of the soil, and full of the thoughts and sentiments as well as the dialect of the people. The old grandfather, worn with disease and living in the past light of fervid days, heard his favorite airs of welcome, gathering, and victory, for the Young Chevalier sung to new and glowing words, and the young ladies laughed at the funny lilts in which were drawn the queer figures of the dullards and provincial fops, without knowing to whose keen pen they were indebted. The Land o' the Leal was written for Mrs. Archibald Campbell Colquhoun, a dear friend of Miss Oliphant, upon the death of an infant daughter, and to one other only was the secret of its authorship ever definitely disclosed, although its aurora, more or less mysteriously, finally settled around the head of Lady Nairne. Mrs. Colquhoun was born Mary Anne Erskine, and was the sister of that William Erskine afterward Lord Kinedder who was the dearest friend and associate of Walter Scott in his early Edinburgh days, and the sister, who kept the house for her brother until her marriage with Mr. Colquhoun, was the earliest and deepest love of Scott.

Somewhat late in life Carolina Oliphant married her cousin, Major William Nairne, the heir to the forfeited Barony of Nairne, Assistant Inspector-

General of Barracks in Scotland, and with him removed to Edinburgh, where she occupied for a time a cottage at Portobello and afterward official quarters in Holyrood place. The impulse given by Burns to the cultivation of native Scotch poetry still continued, and was being strengthened by his contributions of songs for the music of the old airs in Johnson's Museum, and a coterie of the literary ladies of Edinburgh established the Scotch Minstrel for the same purpose. To this Mrs. Nairne became a contributor, with a single friend for a confidant, under the name of "Mrs. Bogan of Bogan," with other pseudonyms, a disguised handwriting and other elaborate precautions for concealment. There was, of course, a keen curiosity to discover the author of these beautiful songs, but the secret was well guarded, and not even the husband was aware of it. "I dare not even tell William"— Mrs. Nairne wrote to her friend — "lest he blab." She and her friend at one time cherished the purpose of "cleansing and moralizing" the songs of Burns, as he had done those of his unknown predecessors, but a wiser second thought restrained them. Miss Oliphant had been "converted," as the phrase goes, when a young woman on a visit to England, and her piety and religious feeling deepened with her years, until it took on completely the rigid, depressing, and dismal forms of Scotch denominationalism, and her genius for poetry shriveled under it. During the visit of George the Fourth to Edinburgh he signalized his theatrical clemency by a restoration of the forfeited titles of the Jacobite nobility, and Major Nairne became Baron Nairne. Lord Nairne survived his restoration but a few years, and died in 1829, leaving his widow with an only son. To his education she devoted herself, residing for a time in Bath, afterward in Ireland, and traveling on the Continent for the health of the young lord, who was of feeble constitution, and who died at Brussels in 1837. It is painful to read of the narrow bigotry and theological gloom which enveloped the joyous and healthy spirit of Lady Nairne. She would not allow her son to be taught to dance, and regarded her poetry as the somewhat flagitious exercise of a worldly spirit, and spent her days in the doubt and self-affliction of a harsh creed and in the petty interests of a narrow church. She was deeply interested in the hopeless task of "converting" the Catholics of Ireland and the Jews to Scotch Presbyterianism, and was the mentor of her relatives after the fashion of Mrs. Hannah More, the patroness of bazaars, and at one time with her sister was expelled from an Italian town for distributing Protestant Bibles to the people. But her native nobleness of character shone through the theological clouds. She was regarded with affection as well as reverence by her younger relatives and her servants, and impressed all who came in contact with her by the cordial grace of her manners, and the aristocratic and highly marked contour of her features, which in the bloom of youth had made her "the Flower of Strathearn." Her benevolence was unceasing and self-sacrificing, if not always wisely directed, and at one time she had all her family plate sold and the proceeds sent to Dr. Chalmers for the support of an industrial school for the poor. She lived during her later years at the old house of Gask, the honored guest of her nephew and his wife, and died in 1845 at the advanced age of seventy-one, in peace and tranquillity, and with only the gentle decay of her mental faculties and bodily forces. The year after her death her poems were collected and published under her own name, and the world for the first time knew to whom it was indebted for the songs which had impressed themselves upon the popular heart and become a distinct and notable part of the lyric poetry of Scotland.

As has been said, The Land o' the Leal reaches the highest note in its inspiration, perfection, and completeness, within the limits of its purpose, not only of Lady Nairne's work, but of all the lyric poetry of Scotland, but it was not the solitary example of a genius which had much of the versatility, if not the fecundity and strength, of Burns, in interpreting the emotions and the thoughts, the passions and the humors, of the Scotch people. Lady Nairne's poetical genius was entirely lyric. There was no Cotter's Saturday Night, much less any scene from Poosey Nancy's alehouse, or witch's gathering at Kirk Alloway, in her interpretation of Scotch life, and her voice was only the pure lilt of Scotch song, grave or gay. Without determined literary ambition and the responsibility of a known name, the stimulus of production was not absorbing and lasting, and a good deal of her work was simply occasional, careless, and imperfect. The best, that which will live as long as Scotch song, could be comprised within the limits of a dozen pages. But its quality is of the very highest in inspiration and execution, the pure voice of the lark lilting beneath the blue cloud, the mourning of the croodlin' doo, and the gay warble of the cheery thrush.

Almost as famous in its own and very different way as The Land o' the Leal, and almost as perfect in its execution, the limitation of the true lyric to the simplest and most absolute words, and the complete interpretation of its spirit in the melody, is The Laird of Cockpen. It was written, it is said, to supply proper words to the gay old air of When She cam ben, She bobbit, which being interpreted, means that when she came into the front of the house, she curtsied, and of which the first verse of the imperfect and rather vulgar old song is —

> When she cam' ben, she bobbit,
> When she cam' ben, she bobbit,
> When she cam' ben she kissed Cockpen
> And syne denied that she did it.

But no one can doubt that it was the true picture of a character and incident which had given laughter to Carolina Oliphant and her young friends, and had been the joke of the country-side, ere it lilted itself to the rollicking jig. The commonly printed version of The Laird of Cockpen is injured by the fact that it has two additional verses, contributed by Miss Ferrier, the novelist, which destroy its absolute completeness and perfection of humor as it was written by Lady Nairne.

THE LAIRD OF COCKPEN.

> The laird of Cockpen, he's proud an' he's great;
> His mind is taen up wi' things o' the State.
> He wanted a wife his braw house to keep,
> But favour wi' wooin' was fasheous to seek.
>
> Down by the dyke-side a lady did dwell,
> At his table-head he thought she'd look well,
> M'Clish's ae daughter o' Claverse-ha'-Lee,
> A penniless lass wi' a long pedigree.

His wig was well pouthered, as gude as when new,
His waistcoat was white, his coat it was blue;
He put on a ring, a sword and cock'd hat,
And wha could resist a laird wi' a that.

He took the grey mare and rode cannily,
An' rapped at the yett o' Claverse-ha'-Lee.
"Gae tell Mistress Jean to come speedily ben—
She's wanted to speak wi' the Laird o' Cockpen."

Mistress Jean was makin' the elder-flower wine;
"O, what brings the laird at sic' a like time."
She put off her apron and on her silk gown,
Her mutch wi' red ribbons, and gaed awa' down.

An' when she cam' ben he bowed fu low,
An' what was his errand he soon let her know;
Amazed was the laird when the lady said "Na,"
And wi' a laigh curtsie she turned awa'.

Dumfoundered was he, nae sigh did he gie.
He mounted his mare — he rade cannily.
An' often he thought as he gaed thro' the glen,
She's daft to refuse the laird o' Cockpen.

Only a little less humorous and perfect is Jamie, the Laird, whose doting mother may have persecuted Carolina Oliphant herself, or some of her friends, with the story of his mental and physical perfections until there was this burst of mocking vexation, to the tune of The Rock and the Wee Pickle Tow:—

JAMIE, THE LAIRD.

Send a horse to the water, ye 'll no mak' him drink;
Send a fule to the college, ye 'll no mak' him think;
Send a craw to the surgin, an' still he will craw;
An' the wee laird had nae rummelgumpshion ava;
Yet he is the pride o' his fond mother's e'e;
In body or mind nae faut can she see;
"He 's a fell clever lad an' a bonnie wee man,"
Is aye the beginnin' an' end o' her sang.
   An' oh, she 's a haverin' Lucky, I trow,
   An' oh, she's a haverin' Lucky, I trow.
   "He 's a fell clever lad, an' a bonnie wee man,"
   Is aye the beginnin' an' end o' her sang.

His legs they are bow'd, his e'es they do glee,
His wig, whiles its off, an' when on, its ajee.
He 's braird as he 's long — an' ill-faur'd is he,
A dafter like body I never did see.
An' yet for this cretur she says I am deein';
When that I deny — she 's fear'd at my leein'.
Obliged to pit up wi' the sair defamation,
I 'm liken to dee wi' shame and vexation.
   An' oh, she 's a haverin' Lucky, etc.

An' her clish-ma-clavers gang a' thro' the town,
An' the wee lairdie trows I 'll hang or I 'll drown;
Wi' his gawkie like face yestreen he did say,
"I 'll maybe tak' you, for Bess I 'll no hae,
Nor Mollie, nor Effie, nor long-legged Jeanie,
Nor Nellie, nor Katie, nor skirlin' wee Beenie."
I stoppet my ears, ran off in a fury —
I 'm thinkin' to bring them before Judge and Jury.
   For oh, what a randy old Lucky is she, etc.

Frien's, gie yere advice — I'll follow yere counsel.
Maun I speak to the Provost or honest Town Council?
Or the writers, or lawyers, or doctors? now say,
For the law o' the Lucky I shall and will hae.
The hale town at me are jibbin' an' jeerin',
For a leddy like me it's really past hearin';
The Lucky now maun hae done wi' her claverin',
For I'll no pit up wi' her an' her haverin'.
  For oh, she's a randy, I trow, I trow,
  For oh, she's a randy, I trow, I trow.
"He's a fell clever lad an' a bonnie wee man,"
Is aye the beginnin' an' end o' her sang.

The finest efflorescence of Scotch lyric poetry, which is the richest and finest in the English language, if not in the world, was that of the Jacobite era, and the influence which followed it and inspired the renaissance of Scotch song is the genius of Burns, Hogg, Cunningham, Lady Nairne, and many more of less distinction, who made a galaxy of singers hardly less remarkable in their way, as marking an era in literature, than the dramatists of the Elizabethan age. The genius of folk-song and ballad poetry had always been remarkably developed in Scotland, in comparison, at least, with England, and, in spite of many characteristics among the Lowlanders, worldly thrift, bitter and barren bigotry, and a sort of dourness and hardheadedness, not calculated to encourage sentiment and emotion; and the student of racial distinctions may be inclined to attribute it to the influence of Celtic blood and tradition, creating a vein of sensitiveness, tenderness, and susceptibility to the magic of song and music in the strong and hard fabric of the Saxon character. But from whatever cause the tendency of the native genius was created, its existence was obvious, and from the very earliest time, since song began to be preserved in written words, the quality and quantity of Scotch folk-poetry and folk-music have been remarkable. The native faculty and the inherited tendency were all present when the spark of an inspiration, involving all the elements of patriotism, daring adventure, personal devotion, despair, and lamentation, gave fire to the genius of national poetry. All the incidents and events of the Rebellion of Forty-five, the landing of the young Prince Charles at Moidart with only seven followers, the blaze of fiery loyalty that swept through the Highlands at his call, the extraordinary victories won by the sheer impetus and hand-to-hand onslaughts of the Highland clans, the picturesque entry into Edinburgh and the gallant court of Holyrood, the swift march into England, which seemed at one time to promise to carry the Chevalier into St. James's Palace by its rush, the retreat and disorganization, and finally the woeful slaughter of Culloden, followed by the attainders and executions and the romantic adventures of the Prince in hiding from his hunters among the mountains and islands, all contrived to create themes for song and poetry which have never been surpassed in modern history. The enterprise was as foolish as it was daring, an episode of knight-errantry after the age when success was possible, but it had all the elements of chivalry in its impulse and conduct, and no modern war has been less selfish and sordid, not even the insurrections of Poland or the uprising of the Spanish and German people against Napoleon. The young Chevalier himself, only twenty-four years of age, tall, handsome, and martial, with his flowing yellow hair and Tartan dress, and with the fascination of his race in his manner, his courage, clemency, and misfortune, gave it the personal element so necessary to the highest poetry, and altogether the circumstances and the conditions combined to create an effervescence of popular poetry which has never been surpassed. Its quantity was as remarkable as its quality. The two large volumes of Hogg's Jacobite Relics by no means exhausted the collection of songs in the Lowland dialect, and to this day those in Gaelic are still being discovered by the labors of Professor Blackie and others, as they are yet preserved in the bothies of the Highlands and the islands. The inspiration of the later poets, Burns, Hogg, Cunningham, and

Lady Nairne, was hardly less strong, fed as it was upon the vivid traditions and by the stories and histories of the men living about them, or of their own families, full of all the elements of poetry, and their purpose to vivify and recreate the native song of Scotland must have had its most fertile impulse and material in the Jacobite songs, of which the country is full. In Lady Nairne the ancestral and personal impulse must have been especially strong. Her father and mother had been married in exile; her grandfather had been distinguished for his services as well as for his misfortunes, and upon both sides her family had been notable for more than one generation for its loyalty and its importance in the Scotch struggle for the restoration of the Stuarts. An old ballad says:—

> Gask and Strowan were nae slack,

and letters of thanks and tokens of gratitude from the royal hands were heirlooms of the houses. It was a keen pleasure to the grandfather in his old age to hear the songs and the music which had illumined the unhappy cause, and it is no wonder that the earliest inspiration of the young poetess was from such themes, and her keenest reward to see the blood warming more freely the old man's worn cheeks as she sang the new and stirring words to the old airs, and found the token of her success in his appreciation. The greater portion of her Jacobite songs were composed under this inspiration, and so long as she wrote at all they were her favorite themes. They are among the finest in what may be termed the modern Jacobite songs, unsurpassed by anything of the kind by Burns, Hogg, or Cunningham, and only so by that consummate flower of all Scotch Jacobite poetry by William Glen: —

> A wee bird cam' to our ha' door,

while in the pure singing quality, the lilt and the verse, there is nothing to exceed the power of —

> The news from Moidart cam' yestreen.

The story of The Hundred Pipers an' A' is historically correct in that there were so many musicians of the class attached to the little army of the Prince, and that the Highland lads did dance themselves dry to the pibroch's sound after fording the Esk, but it was not on the advance to Carlisle, but on the retreat from England, and the scene had doubtless been often described by the old laird of Strowan.

THE HUNDRED PIPERS.

> Wi' a hundred pipers an' a', an' a',
> Wi' a hundred pipers an' a', an' a';

We'll up an' gie them a blaw, a blaw,
Wi' a hundred pipers an' a', an' a',
Oh, it's owre the Border awa', awa';
It's owre the Border awa', awa';
We'll on and we'll march to Carlisle ha;
Wi' its yetts, its castle an' a', an' a',
    Wi' a hundred pipers an' a', etc.

Our young sodger lads looked braw, looked braw,
With their tartans, kilts an' a', an' a',
With their bonnets and feathers and glittering gear,
An' pibrochs sounding sweet an' clear.
Will they a' return to their ain dear glen?
Will they a' return, our Hieland men?
Second-sighted Sandy looked fu wae,
An' mothers grat, when they marched away,
    Wi' a hundred pipers, etc.

O, wha' is foremost o' a', o' a';
O, wha' does follow the blaw, the blaw,
Bonnie Charlie, the King o' us a', hurra!
Wi' his hundred pipers an' a', an' a';
His bonnet an' feather he's wavin' high,
His prancin' steed maist seems to fly,
The nor' wind plays wi' his curlin' hair,
While the pipers blew up an' unco flare,
    Wi' a hundred pipers, etc.

The Esk was swollen sae red and sae deep,
But shouther to shouther the brave lads keep,
Two thousand swam o'er to fell English ground,
An' danced themselves dry to the pibroch's sound.
Dumfoundered the English saw — they saw,

Dumfoundered they heard the blaw, the blaw;
Dumfoundered they a' ran awa', awa',
From the hundred pipers an' a', an' a',
 Wi' a hundred pipers an' a', an' a',
 Wi' a hundred pipers an' a', an' a'.
 We'll up an gie them a blaw, a blaw,
 Wi' a hundred pipers an' a', an' a'.

Burns, Hogg, and Lady Nairne all wrote songs to the beautiful air of Charlie is my Darling, embodying in each case the first verse of the unknown poet who originated the song. They are all beautiful, but the words of Lady Nairne have conquered in the popular ear, and taken final possession of the air.

CHARLIE IS MY DARLING.

'T was on a Monday morning,
 Right early in the year,
When Charlie cam' to our town,
 The young Chevalier.
  Oh, Charlie is my darling,
   My darling, my darling,
  Oh, Charlie is my darling,
   The young Chevalier.

As he cam' marching up the street
 The pipes played loud an' clear,
An' a' the folks cam' running out
 To meet the Chevalier.

Wi' Hieland bonnets on their heads,
 An' claymores bright an' clear,

They cam' to fight for Scotland's right
 An' the young Chevalier.

They 've left their bonnie Highland hills,
 Their wives and bairnies dear,
To draw the sword for Scotland's lord,
 The young Chevalier.

Oh, there were mony beating hearts
 An' mony a hope an' fear,
An' mony were the prayers sent up
 For the young Chevalier.
   Oh, Charlie is my darling,
    My darling, my darling,
   Oh, Charlie is my darling,
    The young Chevalier.

There is one of Lady Nairne's songs not quite perfect, for one forced and faulty line in the refrain, which has a higher touch of the imagination than any of the others. The influence of the magic of nature in the interpretation of human sorrow or gladness, and the wild mystery of the birds' melody upon the heart, which is characteristic of the highest order of the folk-song, and which, in its irregularity and simplicity, not less than the melody, which is nature's own voice, rather than the rhythm of art, is beyond the reach of any deliberate skill. It would be hard to find anything more perfect at once in its picture and its interpretation of the voice of nature in human words than —

And then the burnie's like the sea,
   Roarin' an' reamin';
Nae wee bit sangster's on the tree,
   But wild birds screamin'.

While the sadness of human despair that follows and emphasizes the passion of the flood strikes the ear like a veritable wail in the loneliness and darkness.

Bonnie ran the burnie down,
   Wandrin' an' windin'.
Sweetly sang the birds above,
   Care never mindin'.

The gentle summer wind
   Was their music saft an' kind,
And it rockit them an' rockit them
   All in their bowers sae hie.
      Bonnie ran, etc.

The mossy rock was there,
   An' the water lily fair,
An' the little trout would sport about
   All in the sunny beam.
      Bonnie ran, etc.

Tho' summer days be lang,
   An' sweet the birdies sang,
The wintry night and chilly light
   Keep aye their eerie roun'.
      Bonnie ran, etc.

> An' then the burnie's like a sea,
>   Roarin' an' reamin';
> Nae wee bit sangster's on the tree,
>   But wild birds screamin'.
>
> Oh, that the past I might forget,
>   Wandrin' an' weepin';
> Oh, that aneath the hillock green
>   Sound I were sleepin'.

In one other famous song, heard wherever Scotch music is sung, Lady Nairne interpreted the pathos, hardship, and suffering behind the strong, clear voices of the Newhaven fishwives, which may still be heard in the wynds and closes of Edinburgh as they march on their sturdy limbs with the heavy creels laden with the silvery fishes on their backs, and fill the air with their deep, melodious cry.

CALLER HERRIN'.

> Wha'll buy my caller herrin'?
> They're bonnie fish and halesome farin',
> Wha'll buy my caller herrin',
>   New drawn frae the Forth.
>
> When ye were sleepin' on your pillows,
> Dream'd ye aught o' our fine fellows,
> Darkling as they faced the billows
> A' to fill the woven willows.
>   Buy my caller herrin',
>   New drawn frae the Forth.

Wha 'll buy my caller herrin' ?
They 're no bought without brave darin' ;
Buy my caller herrin',
Haled thro' wind and rain.
   Wha 'll buy my caller herrin' ? etc.

Wha 'll buy my caller herrin' ?
Oh, ye may call them vulgar farin' ;
Wives and mithers maist despairin'
Ca' them the lives o' men.
   Wha 'll buy my caller herrin' ?
   They 're bonnie fish and halesome farin',
   Wha 'll buy my caller herrin',
   New drawn frae the Forth.

There are other verses to Caller Herrin', but they were merely occasional, intended to serve as a benefit to Nathaniel Gow, the son of the famous fiddler, Niel Gow, the composer of the air, who was seeking patronage in Edinburgh, and they only injure the effect of the first and perfect stanzas.

The poetical work of Lady Nairne was smaller in bulk than that of her chief contemporaries, even than that of Allan Cunningham. She was without any personal literary ambition whatever, and her inspiration was smothered by domestic grief and an absorbing and narrow piety. A portion of what there is is also imperfect, ephemeral, and careless, but she has written one of the most perfect lyrics in the English language, and a number of others, which, in their melody, their interpretation of simple emotion, their vividness and strength, and their power upon the heart as well as the ear, have a place which few have equaled and none have surpassed in the lyric treasures of a land more rich than all others in the voice of poetry speaking to the heart in song.

SIR SAMUEL FERGUSON AND CELTIC POETRY.

THE great controversy over the genuineness of the Ossianic poems of James Macpherson, which existed during his lifetime and was carried on for a considerable period after his death, has died away without being settled. Opinions of eminent Celtic scholars still differ as to whether the so-called Gaelic originals of his poems, published after his death, were genuine transcripts from ancient poems, or were translations into the Gaelic from Macpherson's English composition made by his friends to conceal the fraud and maintain provincial pride. He himself never produced the originals of his poems, and took refuge in a silence which went far to confirm the impression of fraud and forgery. But whether he had any direct originals or not, and the weight of probability is that he had not, his poems were unquestionably founded on the vast mass of Celtic poetry and legend existing in Ireland and Scotland in tradition and manuscript. The names of his heroes, their characters and their exploits, are to be found in this poetry, and many of his most admired episodes and descriptions, like that of Ossian's address to the sun, and the description of Cuchullin's chariot, were taken directly from it. Whatever the amount of transformation and interpolation, and whatever the change in the literary style, from the plain and simple expressions of primitive poetry to the vague and rhetorical imagery of inflated artifice, were made by Macpherson, he unquestionably preserved the pervading spirit of Celtic poetry, its melancholy, its sensitiveness to the impressions of nature, and its lofty and humane spirit, and was the first to make it known to the world. Critics like Hazlitt and Matthew Arnold, who were impressed simply by its spirit of pure poetry, and the most accomplished Celtic scholars of a later day, have alike agreed upon internal and external evidence as to the faithfulness of the reproduction of the spirit of Celtic poetry by Macpherson, and have regarded the faults of his literary style as those of the age, and his interpretation of the poems of Ossian by the spirit of the eighteenth century as not more faulty or less natural than Chapman's transfusion of Homer into the style of the Elizabethan era, or Pope's into that of Queen Anne. His great drawback was the suspicion of absolute fraud and forgery which attached to him, and which he was unable to dispel, from his mistake in not acknowledging in the beginning that his poems were derived from general tradition instead of being absolute translations from originals. But in spite of this discredit, which was more of a personal literary quarrel than a critical attack upon the quality of the poetry itself, its value was at once instinctively recognized as a new and original revelation, as an appeal to sensibilities in human nature which had been stifled by the narrow and dry reasoning of English and Continental poetry at the time, and as a breath from the wide air of nature itself. It touched the European spirit, then struggling to emancipate itself from the swaddling bands of authority and artificial society, with electric power, and was a powerful influence in the emancipation both of literature and human action. Ossian profoundly affected the intellectual awakening of Goethe and was a favorite with Napoleon, and throughout the whole of Europe its spirit was an inspiring and governing force. In English literature its effect was not less powerful, although less openly acknowledged owing to the discredit created by the charges of forgery, and both Byron's melancholy and Wordsworth's appreciation of the soul of nature were derived from this pervading spirit of ancient Celtic poetry.

So far as the direct study of Celtic poetry was concerned the Ossianic controversy was unquestionably a misfortune. It threw a cloud of suspicion and discredit upon the genuine fragments which remained, and discouraged the study which might otherwise have been given to them, so that, unquestionably, some traditional Celtic poetry has been lost by the decay of the language as a living speech, and it is only in later years that enlightened scholarship and patriotic feeling have led to the careful and appreciative study of the manuscript volumes which have survived time and neglect, for their inherent literary and historical value, and to a consideration of the influence of the Celtic spirit upon English literature. They have been found to be of great value and interest, to possess elements of pure poetry of marked and original quality, and a spirit which has had a strong effect upon English literature. Nevertheless there has not been found in the remains of Celtic literature any single poem which in itself would compare with the Nibelungen Lied or with the Song of Roland, in epic form and constructiveness, in clearness of diction and dramatic strength; nor even any prose legend or narrative history, which would compare with the clear and vigorous character drawing and lucid narration of the Icelandic and Scandinavian Sagas. What would have been the case had the original poems and histories of the sixth century been preserved can only be conjectured. Those which now exist are only in the transcripts of the eleventh, twelfth, and thirteenth centuries, greatly transformed, altered, and confused in dates and characters, and bearing the marks of a great deterioration in style, like the degradation of Latin prose in its later era. The passages which competent Celtic scholars have pronounced from philological evidence to be of an earlier construction, are a good deal stronger as well as simpler in expression than those by which they are surrounded, and indicate that, if the earlier poetry had been preserved in its purity without being amplified and weakened by scholastic and artificial phraseology, it might have rivaled the early Teutonic poetry in force, directness and simplicity, and strength of construction. As it is, the Celtic poems and histories are not only confused and prolix with interminable genealogies and proverbial reflections, but are written in a style, with a redundance and complication of epithets, at once weakening and tiresome. Thus in an Irish history of the Triumphs of Turlogh O'Brien, written in the thirteenth century, there is the following description of the dress and arms of a hero: —

"His noble garment was first brought to him, viz., a strong, well-formed, close-ridged, defensively-furrowed, terrific, neat-bordered, new-made, and scarlet-red cassock of fidelity; he expertly put on that gold-bordered garment, which covered him as far as from the lower part of his soft, fine, red-white neck, to the upper part of his expert, snow-white, round-knotted knee. Over that mantle he put on a full, strong, white-topped, wide-round, gold-bordered, straight, and parti-colored coat of mail, well-fitted, and ornamented with many curious devices of exquisite workmanship. He put on a beautiful, thick, and saffron-colored belt of war, embellished with clasps and buckles set with precious stones, and hung with golden tassels; to this belt was hung his active and trusty lance, regularly cased in a tubic sheath, but that it was somewhat greater in height than the height of the sheath; he squeezed the brilliant, gilt, and starry belt about the coat of mail; and a long, blue-edged, bright-steeled, sharp-pointed, broad-sided, active, white-backed, half-polished, monstrous, smooth-bladed, small-thick, and well-fashioned dagger was fixed to the tie of that embroidered and parti-colored belt; a white, embroidered, full-wide, strong, and well-wove hood was put on him over his golden mail; he himself laid on his head a strong-cased, spherical, towering, polished-shining, branch-engraved, long-enduring helmet; he took his edged, smooth-bladed, letter-graved, destructive, sharp-pointed, fight-taming, sheathed, gold-guarded, and girded sword, which he tied fast in haste to his side."

The confusion which exists in the transcripts of the ancient poems between the pagan mythology and the Christian faith, and the superposition of

Latin learning and mediæval thought, is also a great injury to the consecutiveness and vraisemblance of the story, and the effect is as if the tale of the Nibelungen Lied had been told by a monkish chronicler with all the embellishments of a later faith and the ornaments of an artificial style. The poetry has not all perished from the earlier originals, and in many instances there is a vigor of narrative, a poetical power of description, and an elevation of sentiment, which shines through the amplification and verbiage, and redeems the prolixity and tediousness of the story; but, as has been said, the prevailing impression is one of a corrupted and weakened, instead of a strong and original primitive poetry, and a literal translation of an Irish or Scotch Celtic poem or history is not likely to attract the general reader from its purely literary quality. The poetry lies in a heap of dross, and must be painfully smelted out.

The only way in which ancient Celtic poetry can be known and appreciated by the English reader, and have its effect in English literature, is by the presentation of its spirit and atmosphere, its essential elements in local form and color, its characteristic phraseology and tone of thought in English poetry of original power as well as essential faithfulness. The poet who is to do this successfully must have, what Macpherson had not, a thorough knowledge of the language and an appreciation of its method as the expression of thought, be completely saturated with the knowledge of the time, and possess the literary conscience and taste to be completely faithful to the original spirit. The most conspicuous example in our time of an attempt to reproduce the spirit of legendary romance in original poetry is, of course, The Idylls of the King, and the impress of a very thorough study and saturation of the spirit of the ancient chronicles is as visible as the exquisite substance of original poetry. But the stories of The Idylls of the King are based upon, rather than closely reproduce, the legends of Arthurian romance, and the spirit has been elevated and refined by that of modern poetry and the nature of Tennyson's own genius to essential unreality. They are like the pictures of Madonnas and mediæval saints done by a modern painter of genius with all the skill and technique of art, but without the sense of devotion which shows through the ruder sketches of the earlier and greatly inferior painters, who were inspired by something more than merely artistic enthusiasm. It is needless to say that for a poet to possess the self-restraint to be entirely faithful to his originals, and aim mainly at reproducing their form as well as spirit, is more rare, and may be said to have less power, than one who creates an original structure of poetry upon the basis of ancient romance; but he has his function also, and may be something more than a mere translator, as he gives his material shape in modern form and with the embellishments of his own genius, while he yet preserves the ancient characteristics. He is like the skillful architect who restores a ruined castle to a habitable dwelling, clearing away the rubbish which has choked its portals and surrounded its walls, while preserving its ancient shape and structure, and blending his new materials with the old so that it seems a harmonious building. This is the work to which Sir Samuel Ferguson has devoted himself in his reproduction of Irish Celtic poetry, both ballad and epic, and particularly in his poem of Congal, which is a recreation of the bardic romance of the Battle of Moyra, and its introductory Pre-Tale of the Banquet of Dunangay, prose versions which have been given by the eminent Celtic scholar, Dr. John O'Donovan, in the publications of the Irish Archæological Society.

The battle of Moyra was an authentic historic event, and took place A. D. 637 between the forces of Domnal, king of Ireland, and those of Congal, sub-king of Ulster, and his allies from Scotland, Wales, England, Brittany, and Scandinavia. It is regarded by Celtic historians as the last struggle of the bardic and pagan party in Ireland against the newly established power of Christianity, for which a pretext rather than a cause was found in an alleged slight of Domnal to Congal. The history, which is in prose interspersed with speeches and exhortations in verse in the usual manner of the bardic chronicles, was apparently written in its present form in the latter part of the eleventh century, and from earlier traditionary chronicles, which are now lost. Its style has a good deal of vigor and force, but is marked with the faults of confusion, and the redundance of descriptive epithets characteristic of the writers of the time. Its story is that Congal, having been invited by Domnal to a banquet at the royal house at Dunangay, was served with a hen's egg upon a wooden platter, instead of with a goose egg upon a silver dish, as were the remainder of the company, and, denouncing it as an unforgivable insult, departed to seek assistance from his relatives and allies in Great Britain and the Continent. Returning with these a great battle was fought on the plains of Moyra, which lasted for six days, and in which the foreign invaders were routed and Congal was killed. The principal heroes of the chronicle were historical personages, but there were others of which there is no definite knowledge, and who probably owed their origin to the imagination of the bards, as in the Iliad and the Nibelungen Lied. Sir Samuel Ferguson's poem of Congal follows the main narrative of events in the original chronicle, but with an addition in the shape of a love episode between Lafinda, a sister of Sweeny, an Irish prince, and Congal, the introduction of several new characters, and of some supernatural episodes derived from the pagan mythology of Ireland. The narrative is made intelligible where it is obscure in the original, and incredible events, such as the chaining together of the warriors lest they should run away from each other, are omitted, while the tautology and verbiage of the language is eliminated. Its faithfulness as the reproduction of an ancient Celtic poem consists in the skill with which the characteristic style of language, its multiplied and doubled epithets, is renewed in English without the effect of archaism, and the reproduction of its heroic and primitive tone and spirit. Its original merits are the force and vigor of the narrative, the vivid descriptions of scenery, the strength and impressiveness of the supernatural figures, the genuine inspiration of battle in the combats, and the easy mastery of the "long, resounding line" in the verse. There is no modern poem which so thoroughly reproduces the ancient form and spirit of a bygone age, and in which so complete and accurate an idea can be obtained of the element of a vanished poetry as in Congal, and, as has been said, it is like a restoration in shape and substance of a ruined castle. The opening lines give a specimen of the style of the verse and the vigorous spirit of the measure : —

The Hosting here of Congal Claen. 'T was loud lark-car-
    oling May
When Congal, as the lark elate and radiant as the day,
Rode forth from steep Rath-Keltar gate.

Of the felicity with which these double descriptive epithets are used there are a thousand specimens, such as

    The white-maned, proud-neck-arching tide ;

and they give the dominant characteristic of the style as in the original, with a grace and appropriateness which make them a natural part of the English language. In order to show how the Celtic narrative has been transformed into English poetry without losing its characteristic features, the two accounts of the episode in the battle in which Sweeny becomes smitten with a frenzy of fear by supernatural visitation may be compared. This is the original : —

"Fits of giddiness came over him at *the sight* of the horrors, grimness, and rapidity of the Gaels; at the looks, brilliance, and irksomeness of the foreigners ; at the rebounding, furious shouts and bellowings of the various embattled tribes on both sides, rushing against and coming into collision with one another. Huge, flickering, horrible, aerial phantoms rose up, so that they were in curved, commingled crowds tormenting him; and in dense, rustling, clamorous, life-tormenting hordes, without ceasing; and in dismal, regular, aerial, storm-shrieking, hovering, fiend-like hosts, constantly in motion, shrieking and howling as they hovered about them in every direction, to cow and dismay cowards and soft youths, but to invigorate and mightily rouse champions and warriors; so that from the uproar of the battle, the frantic pranks of the demons, and the clashing of arms, the sound of heavy blows reverberating on the points of heroic spears, and keen edges of swords, and the war-like borders of broad shields, the noble hero Suibne was filled and intoxicated with tremor, horror, panic, dismay, fickleness, unsteadiness, fear, flightiness, giddiness, terror, and imbecility; so that there was not a joint or member of him from foot to head which was not converted into a confused, shaking mass, from the effect of fear and the panic of dismay. His feet trembled as if incessantly shaken by the force of a stream; his arms and various-edged weapons fell from him, the power of his hands having been enfeebled and relaxed around them, and rendered incapable of holding them. The inlets of hearing were quickened and expanded by the horrors of lunacy; the vigor of his brain in the cavities of his head was destroyed by the clamors of the conflict; his heart shrunk within him with the panic of dismay; his speech became faltering from the giddiness of imbecility; his very soul fluttered with hallucination, and with many and various phantoms, for that was the root and true basis of fear itself. He might be compared on this occasion to a salmon in a weir, or to a bird after being caught in the strait prison of a crib."

The following is the way in which this is rendered in Congal, Sweeny's offense having consisted in drowning the hermit Erc in the Boyne: —

To Sweeny as the hosts drew near, ere yet the fight should join,
Seemed still, as if between them rolled the foam-strewed, tawny Boyne.
And as the swiftly nearing hosts consumed the narrowing space,
And arrow flights and javelin casts, and sword strokes came in place,
Through all the rout of high-raised hands, and wrathful, glaring eyes,
Erc's look of wrath, and lifted hand before him seemed to rise,
Through all the hard-rebounding din from breasts of Gaels and Gauls,
That jarred against the vault of heaven, when clashed the brazen walls,
Through all the clangorous battle-calls, and death shouts hoarse and high,

Ere's shriller curse he seemed to hear and Ere's despairing
    cry.
Much did the hapless warrior strive to shake from breast
    and brain
The illusion and the shameful wish fast-rising; but in vain;
The wish to fly seized all his limbs; the stronger dread of
    shame,
Contending with the wish to fly, made spoil of all his frame.
His knees beneath him wavered as if shaken by the stress
Of a rapid running river; his heart, in fear's excess,
Sprang to and fro within him, as a wild bird newly caged,
Or a stream-ascending salmon in a strong weir's trap en-
    gaged.

Some of the single combats of the heroes, following the details of the narrative, are described with Homeric vigor, and the address of the King of Lochlan to the invading army, disheartened by apparitions, has the fire and spirit, as well as the form, of the Scandinavian runic verse: —

    This is my sentence:
    Fairy nor Fire-Drake
    Keep back the Kemper
    At home, in the burg,
    Leaves he the maiden
    Boon for the bridal;
    Abroad, on the holme,
    Leaves he the harvest,
    Ripe for the reaper;
    The bowl, on the board,
    In the hall of the banquets,
    Leaves he untasted,

When lances uplift
The foe in the field.
Noting the Norsemen
Out on the water-throng,
Hark! how the Eagle
Vaunts to the Vulture.
Spread the wing, Scald-Neck,
Says she, and screams she;
Seest thou the Sea-Kings
Borne on the gannet-bath,
Going to garner
Every bird's eyrie?
Fell from her fishy-perch
Answers the Bald-Beak,
Scream no more, little one,.
Feeders are coming.
Hearkening their colloquy,
Grins the grey beast,
The wolf on the wold.
This is my sentence:
These are the Norseman's
Pandect and canon.
Thyrfing is thirsty;
Quern-biter hungers;
Shield-walker wearieth
Shut in the scabbard.
This is my sentence:
Bring us to battle.

Perhaps, however, the greatest strength in Congal will be found in the dealing with the apparitions, the gigantic and malign demons, who haunt the hill and the stream, and represent the primitive imaginings of a race not yet emancipated from the terrors of the supernatural in the forces and forms of nature. These figures of ancient Irish poetry, the Herdsman Borcha, who swept down Finn's fortress with his staff, and counts the kine in the unconquered lands, the Giant Walker, who strides angrily around the hostile camp at night, and the Washer at the Ford, who dabbles with slain men's heads, live again in Ferguson's verse with their original reality and terror, and amid the setting of natural scenery from which their phantoms were created. This is the picture of the Giant Walker, whose apparition presaged doom to Cougal at his first night's camp:—

    Around the Mound of Sighs
They filled the woody-sided vale ; but no sweet sleep their
  eyes
Refreshed that night ; for all the night, around their echo-
  ing camp,
Was heard continuous from the hills a sound as of a tramp
Of giant footsteps ; but so thick the white mist lay around
None saw the Walker save the King. He, starting at the
  sound,
Called to his foot his fierce red hound ; athwart his shoulders
  cast
A shaggy mantle, grasped his spear, and through the moon-
  light passed
Alone up dark Ben-Boli's heights, towards which, above the
  woods,
With sound as when at close of eve the noise of falling floods
Is borne to shepherd's ear remote on stilly upland lawn,

The steps along the mountain-side with hollow sound came on.
Fast beat the hero's heart ; and close, down-crouching by his knee
Trembled the hound, while through the haze, huge as through mists at sea,
The week-long sleepless mariner descries some mountain cape,
Wreck-infamous, rise on his lee, appeared a monstrous shape
Striding impatient, like a man much grieved, who walks alone
Considering of a grievous wrong ; down from his shoulders thrown
A mantle skirted stiff with soil, splashed from the miry ground,
At every stride against his calves struck with as loud rebound
As makes the mainsail of a ship brought up along the blast,
When with the coil of all its ropes it beats the sounding mast.
So, striding vast, the giant passed ; the King held fast his breath ;
Motionless save his throbbing heart ; and still and chill as death
Stood listening while a second time the giant took his round
Of all the camp ; but when, at length, the third time the sound
Came up, and through the haze a third time huge and dim
Rose out the Shape, the valiant hound sprang forth and challenged him.
And forth, disdaining that a dog should put him so to shame,
Sprang Congal and essayed to speak.

"Dread shadow, stand ! Proclaim
What wouldst thou that thou thus around my camp shouldst keep

Thy troublous vigil, banishing the wholesome gift of sleep
From all our eyes, who, though inured to dreadful sounds
    and sights
By land and sea, have never yet in all our perilous nights
Lain the ward of such a guard."
                          The Shape made answer none,
But with stern wafture of his hand went angrier striding on,
Shaking the earth with heavier steps. Then Congal on his
    track
Sprang fearless.
    "Answer me, thou Churl," he cried, "I bid thee back."
But, while he spoke, the giant's cloak around his shoulders
    grew
Like a black-bulged thunder-cloud; and sudden out there
    flew
From all its angry, swelling folds, with uproar unconfined,
Direct against the King's pursuit a mighty blast of wind:
Loud flapped the mantle, tempest-lined, while fluttering
    down the gale,
As leaves in Autumn, man and hound were swept into the vale,
And heard through all the huge uproar, through startled
    Dalaray,
The giant went with stamp and clash, departing south away.

A conspicuous feature of the excellence of Congal as an original poem is the vividness and faithfulness with which the natural scenery of Ireland is painted. The dark and barren hills, the tawny and foam-flecked streams, the misty seas, the vast and lonely raths and burial places of heroes, the emerald fields bathed with dew and glittering with sunshine, all the characteristics of Irish scenery, with their soul of meaning, which appeals to the heart as well as the outward form to the eye, are depicted with remarkable power, and make a living element in which the figures move. Almost every page has a touch of this skill, and every aspect of field and sea and sky is enlivened. As fine a specimen as any is this picture of an autumn champaign from a hill-top in Leinster : —

       Such as one
Beholds, and thankful-hearted he, who casts abroad his gaze
O'er some rich tillage country-side, when mellow autumn
   days
Gild all the sheafy food-full stooks, and, broad before him
   spread, —
He looking landward from the prow of some great sea-cape's
   head
Bray or Ben-Edar — sees beneath in silent pageant grand
Slow fields of sunshine spread o'er fields of rich, corn-bearing
   land ;
Red glebe and meadow-margin green commingling to the
   view,
With yellow stubble, browning woods, and upland tracts of
   blue ; —
Then, sated with the pomp of fields, turns seaward to the
   verge
Where, mingling with the murmuring wash made by the
   far-down surge,
Comes up the clangorous song of birds unseen, that, low be-
   neath
Poised off the rock, fly underfoot, and, mid the blossoming
   heath,

And mint-sweet herb that loves the ledge rare-aired, at ease
    reclined,
Surveys the wide, pale-heaving floor crisped by a curling
    wind ;
With all its shifty shadowing belts, and chasing scopes of
    green,
Sun strown, foam-freckled, sail-embossed, and blackening
    squalls between,
And slant, cerulean-skirted showers, that with a drowsy
    sound,
Heard inward, of ebullient waves, stalk all the horizon round.

With its faithfulness to tone and character, its skillful reproduction of style and language, its force and vigor of narrative, its forms of mythologic mysticism and its appreciation of the magic of nature, Congal is the most perfect reproduction of the form and spirit of ancient Celtic poetry in existence, and from it the English reader, who is not a Celtic student, can obtain the best knowledge of its pervading elements.

Congal is not the only contribution made by Sir Samuel Ferguson to Celtic poetry. The Lays of the Western Gael are a series of ballads founded on events in Celtic history and derived from the early chronicles and poems. They are original in form and substance, the ballad form and measure being unknown to the early Celtic poets of Ireland, but they preserve in a wonderful degree the ancient spirit, and give a picture of the ancient times with all the art of truth and verity. As I have said elsewhere [1]: —

"To have done this clearly and completely, so that the past lives again and is felt by the instinct of nature to be true and real, free from confusion and extravagance, the imperfections of utterance in a people just learning to express themselves, the alien and antique methods of thought, through the inevitably imperfect knowledge of a language half faded and changed, while preserving not only the terms of expression but the characteristics of thought and feeling, seems a no less difficult task than to trace and interpret the worn letters and half-effaced inscriptions on the Ogham stones, and could only have been done by the genius of the great poet vivifying the labor of the profound scholar. Finally, the impress of the past as it is visible to the present, the effect of the gray cairn and grassy burial mound, and almost the last fading of the tokens of the aboriginal race into the bosom of nature, and the perception of its spirit amid the light and bustle of the day,

>The loneliness and awe secure

of the forgotten dead, is the task of the modern poet speaking in his own time and to his own generation of the past."

[1] Introduction to popular edition of *Lays of the Western Gael*, Dublin, 1888.

These ballads have a solemnity of measure like the voice of one of the ancient bards chanting of

> Old, forgotten, far-off things
> And battles long ago,

and they are clothed with the mists of a melancholy age. They include such subjects as The Tain Quest, the search of the bard for the lost lay of the great cattle raid of Queen Maev of Connaught, and its recovery by invocation from the voice of its dead author arising in misty form above his grave; The Healing of Conall Carnach, a story of violated sanctuary and its punishment; The Welshmen of Tyrawly, one of the most spirited and original, and which has been pronounced by Mr. Swinburne as among the finest of modern ballads, telling of a cruel mulct inflicted upon the members of a Welsh colony in Ireland and its vengeance, and other incidents in early Irish history. The verses on Aideen's Grave are a characteristic specimen of the tone and spirit of these ballads. The author's introductory note says:—

"Aideen, daughter of Angus of Ben Edar (now the Hill of Howth), died of grief for the loss of her husband Oscar, son of Ossian, who was slain at the battle of Gavra (Gowra near Tara in Meath) A. D. 284. Oscar was entombed in the rath, or earthen fortress, that occupied part of the field of battle, the rest of the slain being cast in a pit outside. Aideen is said to have been buried on Howth, near the mansion of her father, and poetical tradition represents the Fenian heroes as present at her obsequies. The cromlech in Howth Park is supposed to have been her sepulchre."

AIDEEN'S GRAVE.

They heaved the stones ; they heaped the cairn.
    Said Ossian, " In a queenly grave
We leave her, 'mong her fields of fern
    Between the cliff and wave."

The cliff behind stands clear and bare,
    And bare, above, the heathery steep
Scales the clear heaven's expanse, to where
    The Danaan Druids sleep.

And all the sands that, left and right,
    The grassy isthmus-ridge confine,
In yellow bars lie bare and bright
    Among the sparkling brine.

A clear pure air pervades the scene,
    In loneliness and awe secure,
Meet spot to sepulchre a Queen,
    Who in her life was pure.

Here far from camp and chase removed,
    Apart in Nature's quiet room,
The music that alive she loved
    Shall cheer her in the tomb.

The humming of the noontide bees,
   The lark's loud carol all day long,
And, borne on evening's salted breeze,
   The clanking sea-birds' song

Shall round her airy chamber float,
   And with the whispering winds and streams,
Attune to Nature's tenderest note
   The tenor of her dreams.

And oft at tranquil eve's decline,
   When full tides lap the Old Green Plain,
The lowing Moynalty's kine
   Shall round her breathe again.

In sweet remembrance of the days
   When, duteous in the lowly vale,
Unconscious of my Oscar's gaze,
   She filled the fragrant pail.

And, duteous, from the running brook,
   Drew water for the bath; nor deem'd
A king did on her labor look,
   And she a fairy seemed.

But when the wintry frosts begin,
   And in their long-drawn, lofty flight
The wild geese with their airy din
   Distend the ear of night.

And when the fierce De Danaan ghosts,
   At midnight from their peak come down.
When all around the enchanted coasts
   Despairing strangers drown;

When mingling with the wreckful wail
    From low Clontarf's wave-trampled floor,
Comes booming up the burthened gale
    The angry Sand Bull's roar;

Or, angrier than the sea, the shout
    Of Erin's hosts in wrath combined
When Terror heads Oppression's rout
    And Freedom cheers behind : —

Then o'er our lady's placid dream,
    When safe from storms she sleeps, may steal
Such joy as may not misbeseem
    A queen of men to feel.

Such thrill of free, defiant pride,
    As rapt her in her battle car
At Gavra, when by Oscar's side
    She rode the ridge of war.

Exulting, down the shouting troops,
    And through the thick confronting kings,
With hands on all their javelin loops
    And shafts on all their strings;

E'er closed the inseparable crowds
    No more to part for me, and show,
As bursts the sun through scattering clouds
    My Oscar issuing so.

No more, dispelling battle's gloom,
    Shall son to me from fight return;
The great green rath's ten-acred tomb
    Lies heavy on his urn.

A cup of bodkin-pencilled clay
  Holds Oscar ; mighty heart and limb
One handful now of ashes grey :
  And she has died for him.

And here, hard by her natal bower
  On lone Ben-Edar's side we strive
With lifted rock and sign of power
  To keep her name alive.

That, while from circling year to year,
  Her Ogham-lettered stone is seen,
The Gael shall say, " Our Fenians here
  Entombed their loved Aideen.

The Ogham from her pillar stone
  In tract of time will wear away;
Her name at last be only known
  In Ossian's echoed lay.

The long-forgotten lay I sing
  May only ages hence revive,
(As eagle with a wounded wing
  To soar again might strive.)

Imperfect, in an alien speech,
  When, wandering here, some child of chance
Through pangs of keen delight shall reach
  The gift of utterance, —

To speak the air, the sky to speak,
  The freshness of the hill to tell,
When, roaming bare Ben-Edar's peak
  And Aideen's briary dell,

And gazing on the Cromlech vast,
    And on the mountain and the sea,
Shall catch communion with the past
    And mix himself with me.

Child of the Future's doubtful night,
    Whate'er your speech, whoe'er your sires,
Sing while you may with frank delight
    The song your hour inspires.

Sing while you may, nor grieve to know
    The song you sing shall also die;
Atharna's lay has perished so,
    Though once it thrilled the sky.

Above us, from his rocky chair
    There, where Ben-Edar's landward crest
O'er eastern Bregia bends, to where
    Dun-Almon crowns the west:

And all that felt the fretted air,
    Throughout the song-distempered clime,
Did droop, till Leinster's suppliant prayer
    Appeased the vengeful rhyme.

Ah, me, or e'er the hour arrive
    Shall bid my long-forgotten tones,
Unknown One, on your lips revive,
    Here, by these moss-grown stones,

What change shall o'er the scene have cross'd
    What conquering lords anew have come;
What lore-armed, mightier Druid host
    From Gaul or distant Rome!

What arts of death, what ways of life,
  What creeds unknown to bard or seer,
Shall round your careless steps be rife,
  Who pause and ponder here:

And, haply, where yon curlew calls
  Athwart the marsh, 'mid groves and bowers
See rise some mighty chieftain's halls
  With unimagined towers:

And baying hounds and coursers bright,
  And burnish't cars of dazzling sheen,
With courtly train of dame and knight,
  Where now the fern is green.

Or by yon prostrate altar stone
  May kneel, perchance, and free from blame,
Hear holy men with rites unknown
  New names of God proclaim.

Let change as may the name of Awe,
  Let right surcease and altar fall,
The same one God remains, a law
  Forever and for all.

Let change as may the face of earth,
  Let alter all the social frame,
For mortal men the ways of birth
  And death are still the same.

And still, as life and time wear on,
  The children of the waning days
(Though strength be from their shoulders gone
  To lift the loads we raise)

> Shall weep to do the burial rites
>   Of lost ones loved ; and fondly found
> In shadow of the gathering nights
>   The monumental mound.
>
> Farewell, the strength of men is worn ;
>   The night approaches dark and chill ;
> Sleep till, perchance, an endless morn
>   Descend the glittering hill " —
>
> Of Oscar and Aideen bereft
>   So Ossian sang. The Fenians sped
> Three mighty shouts to heaven ; and left
>   Ben-Edar to the dead.

The spirit of Ossian, the woe and desolation of a mortal world, and the resigned but not bitter sense of the vanity of all things, lives in this solemn elegy.

The charming lyrics of the later Irish Celtic poetry, which succeeded that of the bards, and were the voices of the peasant people themselves and of the professional descendants of the bards, the itinerant poets and musicians, who wandered from house to house with their harps, singing the praises of their entertainers, and were not extinct until the end of the last century, have found an adequate interpreter in Sir Samuel Ferguson. As in his reproductions of the bardic poetry, he has been able to seize the very spirit of these songs, their intoxication of love, their breath of hopeless longing and misfortune, the characteristics of the race and the results of their cruel fate at the hands of alien conquerors, and to interpret it in measures as melodious as the sad and sweet old airs, which are the most valuable gift which the intellectual life of Celtic Ireland has bestowed upon posterity. The genuine Irish melodies are to be found in these lyrics, which interpret the spirit as well as the language of the Celtic poets, and not in the rococo songs of Moore, in which artificial sentiment is tricked out in a mechanical melody, and in which the atmosphere of the drawing-room takes the place of the free air of the hillside. Of these Celtic lyrics the greater number have been lost, the airs alone surviving, but those which remain show how strong, sensitive, and impassioned was the poetic spirit of the Irish Celtic people, and which, but for the misfortunes of the nation, might have left as rich a treasury of lyric song as the Scotch. The following is a specimen of the impassioned spirit of these songs, almost an improvisation, the very cry of the heart finding vent at the lips. It is entitled Cean Dubh Deelish — The Dear Black Head.

> Put your head, darling, darling, darling,
>   Your darling black head my heart above;
> Oh, mouth of honey, with the thyme for fragrance,
>   Who with heart in breast could deny you love?
> Oh, many and many a young girl for me is pining,

Letting her locks of gold to the cold wind free,
For me the foremost of our gay young fellows;
But I'd leave a hundred, pure love, for thee :
Then put your head, darling, darling, darling,
Your darling black head my heart above ;
Oh, mouth of honey, with the thyme for fragrance,
Who, with heart in breast, could deny you love?

The verses entitled The Fair Hair'd Girl express with great sweetness the sense of woe and sorrow which forms the burden of so much of the Celtic poetry, and which is only relieved by occasional flashes of intoxicated merriment with the glass of whiskey for its stimulus and inspiration.

THE FAIR HAIR'D GIRL.

The sun has set, the stars are still,
The red moon hides behind the hill ;
The tide has left the brown beach bare,
The birds have fled the upper air ;
Upon her branch the lone cuckoo
Is chanting still her sad adieu ;
And you, my fair hair'd girl, must go
Across the salt sea under woe.

I through love have learned three things,
Sorrow, sin, and death it brings,
Yet day by day my heart within
Dares shame and sorrow, death and sin ;
Maiden, you have aim'd the dart
Rankling in my ruin'd heart ;
Maiden, may the God above
Grant you grace to grant me love.

Sweeter than the viol's string,
And the notes that blackbirds sing;
Brighter than the dewdrops rare
Is the maiden, wondrous fair;
Like the silver swans at play
Is her neck, as bright as day;
Woe is me, that e'er my sight
Dwelt on charms so deadly bright.

Among the sweetest and most famous of the old Irish airs is that entitled The Coolun or Head of Clustering Tresses, one of the charming personifications of female beauty of which Irish poetry is full. Several sets of words remain to this air of which Ferguson has translated the following:—

THE COOLUN.

Oh, had you seen the Coolun,
   Walking down by the cuckoo's street,
With the dew of the meadow shining
   On her milk-white twinkling feet,
My love she is and my *cooleen oge*,
   And she dwells at Bal'nagar;
And she bears the palm of beauty bright
   From the fairest that in Erin are.

In Bal'nagar is the Coolun,
   Like the berry on the bough her cheek;
Bright beauty dwells forever
   On her fair neck and ringlets sleek;
Oh, sweeter is her mouth's soft music
   Than the lark or thrush at dawn,

Or the blackbird in the greenwood singing
    Farewell to the setting sun.

Rise up, my boy, make ready
    My horse, for I forth would ride,
To follow the modest damsel,
    Where she walks on the green hillside.
For, ever since our youth were we plighted,
    In faith, troth, and wedlock true —
She is sweeter to me nine times over
    Than organ or cuckoo!

For, ever since my childhood
    I loved the fair and darling child;
But our people came between us,
    And with lucre our pure love defiled;
Oh, my woe it is, and my bitter pain,
    And I weep it night and day,
That the *cooleen bawn* of my early love
    Is torn from my heart away.

Sweetheart and faithful treasure,
    Be constant still, and true,
Nor for want of herds and houses
    Leave one who would ne'er leave you;
I pledge you the blessed Bible,
    Without and eke within,
That the faithful God will provide for us,
    Without thanks to kith or kin.

Oh, love, do you remember,
    When we lay all night alone,
Beneath the ash in the winter-storm,
    When the oak-wood round did groan?

> No shelter then from the blast had we,
> The bitter blast or sleet,
> But your gown to wrap about our heads,
> And my coat round our feet.

The main literary work of Sir Samuel Ferguson was devoted to this revivification of the spirit of ancient Celtic poetry, in spite of a highly successful début as an English poet in The Forging of the Anchor, which at once took its place among those poems that are the familiar treasures of the people, and in this he was doubtless governed by something of patriotic spirit as well as by natural predilection. His work is not great in quantity, and he treasured his inspiration and perfected his workmanship with careful pains. Its result is to give a reproduction of the pervading elements of Irish Celtic poetry in English form with almost absolute perfection, and imbued with a spirit of original genius. In his poems, rather than in Macpherson's Ossian or in the literal translations, will the modern reader find the voice of the ancient Celtic bards speaking to the intelligence of to-day in their own tones without false change and dilution, or the confusion and dimness of an ancient language. The value of this work has not yet been fully appreciated by literary critics, but there is no doubt in my mind but that it eventually will be,

WILLIAM THOM, THE WEAVER POET.

ONE of the most extraordinary and painful lives in literary history was that of William Thom of Inverury, Scotland. There have been Scottish poets before and since Burns who have been bred in poverty and distress, and in whose lives the flowers of poetry have bloomed amid the most depressing and uncongenial circumstances. There have been crofters, shepherds, farm laborers, tailors, weavers, and shoemakers, servant lassies and old wives, who have given expression to their feelings in verse and song, with more or less skill and success, and testified to the strength of the national genius which has made Scotland so peculiarly the land of song, and filled the lower bed of bracken and furze in which the higher and rarer flowers of Scottish minstrelsy have stood preëminent. And the history of the minor Scottish poets is full of the homely pathos of unrequited toil, of pinching poverty, and of hopeless struggles with life, redeemed by honest virtue, patience, and thrift, or clouded with still deeper misfortune, and absolutely and irredeemably wrecked by dissipation and improvidence. But upon none, in whom the divine spark of genius existed, did the burdens of life fall more heavily than upon William Thom, or the tragedies of existence reach a blacker depth of misery. The story has been told by himself in The Rhymes and Recollections of a Handloom Weaver, his only volume, in nervous and vigorous prose, bearing traits of the declamatory style of Ebenezer Elliot and the radical writers of his school, but marked by native originality and strength. It has more than a personal value, as illustrating the condition of the life of factory hands in Scotland, when machines had multiplied to the complete degradation of labor, and when it was simply a question with the mill owners of extracting the largest amount of work for the smallest wages from the operatives, and before the government had interfered to regulate the hours of labor within endurable limits, and secure some of the conditions of health to the mill hands. A more appalling picture of hopeless poverty and starvation, and physical and moral degradation, has never been given in the annals of the civilized world, and of its truth there is abundant evidence in the writings of contemporary workingmen in England and Scotland, and in the testimony which led to the passage of the Factory Regulation acts by the English Parliament.

William Thom was born in 1798 of parents

steeped in poverty, in a tenement in one of the narrow closes of Aberdeen, and at the age of ten began his apprenticeship to life in a cotton factory. At the age of fifteen or sixteen he entered the "School Hill Factory," — a building since swept away, — as a weaver hand, and remained there for seventeen years. The wages of the best operatives averaged through good and bad times from six to nine shillings weekly, and of the second-class from three to five shillings. The daily hours of labor were fourteen. What that meant, not in poverty, but in absolute want of food, warmth, and the means for the sustenance of life, the degradation of rags, the shutting out of all glimpses of heaven and earth, leaving the only alleviation to the hours of toil at the rattling machines, and the squalid suffering in the reeking tenements, in the cheap and fiery stimulants of the taprooms, can be only faintly imagined. An inheritance of bad habits had also descended to the weaving class. When the factories were first established in 1770, after the invention of the spinning jenny, the wages of skillful workmen were forty shillings a week, and the operatives usually remained drunk from Saturday night until Wednesday morning, wore frilled shirts and powdered hair, sported canes, and quoted Volney in their discussions on the rights of man in the taprooms. The overplus of labor gradually reduced the wages to the starvation point, while the habits of dissipation and recklessness remained as characteristic of the craft. Thom gives a most affecting picture of the lives and thoughts of these men, many of them, strong with native intellect and passion, condemned to a life of unending servitude and degradation, too ragged to dare to enter a church, even if they wished, and getting their only glimpse of nature in the garden of Gordon's Hospital, which was open on the Sunday holiday, while the whiskey shop gave them their only taste of joy and exhilaration; and yet who had a native feeling for poetry, repeating the verses of Burns and particularly of Tannahill, their brother weaver, as they tended their looms, and applauding the poets and singers in their own ranks, whose rude verses expressed their feelings or appealed to their sympathies in the gatherings in the taprooms. The moral influences of such a life, where three or four hundred men and women were herded together in common workrooms was also very bad, and many a young girl dated her ruin in life, bringing additional desolateness to the miserable home, from the promiscuous association, and being barred out into the streets with a heavy fine for failing to be at the factory door at its opening in the early morning. How virtue, morality, or any of the decency and self-respect of humanity could exist at all in such a life may be considered a marvel, and it is a proof of the inherent strength of the Scottish character and its inherited virtues that these factories were not greater plague spots than they actually were, and that honest lives and human affections flourished at all. In a poem, entitled Whisperings to the Unwashed, in the fiercely declamatory style of the Corn Law Rhymer, Thom draws a grim picture of the awakening of the weavers at the call of the town drum, used for that purpose in the smaller burghs, at six o'clock in the bleak and dark Northern mornings.

> Rubadub, rubadub, row-dow-dow!
> Hark how he waukens the Weavers now;
> Who lie belaired in a dreamy steep —
> A mental swither, 'tween death and sleep,
> Wi' hungry wame and hopeless heart,
> Their food no feeding, their sleep no rest;
> Arouse ye, ye sunken, unravel your rags,
> No coin in your coffers, no meal in your bags.
> Yet cart, barge, and wagon, with load after load,
> Creak, mockfully passing your breadless abode.
> The stately stalk of Ceres bears,
> But not for you the bursting ears.
> In vain to you the lark's lov'd note,
> For you no summer breezes float,
> Grim winter through your hovel pours —
> Dull, dim, and breathless vapour yours.
> The nobler Spider weaves alone,
> And feels the little web his own,

His home, his fortress, foul or fair,
No factory whipper swaggers there.
Should ruffian wasp or taunting fly
Touch his lov'd lair, 't is touch and die !
Supreme in rags, ye weave, in tears,
The shining robe your murderer wears,
Till worn at last to the very " waste,"
A hole to die in at the best ;
And, dead, the session saints begrudge ye
The two-three deals in death to lodge ye,
And grudge the grave, wherein to drop ye.
And grudge the very muck to hap ye.

All this bitterness had reason and fact to excuse it, and it is a wonder that such feelings, fermenting in strong minds, did not lead to more serious consequences than taproom talk and the formation of Chartist clubs.

In such surroundings, what was the character and career of Thom himself ? An active mind led him to the perusal of such books as came in his way, and a poetical temperament made him deeply sensitive to the suffering and degradation of his condition, while it gave him a stimulus toward the fleeting pleasures of dissipation and the glow of sociability and popularity among his fellows. He was without the determined energy to rise above his condition, which might have succeeded had an exceptional strength been allied with his mental gifts, in spite of the forlorn circumstances; and he appears to have been, if not content, at least to have submitted to be only the popular genius among the workmen of his factory, and the leader in the taproom gatherings with his social and musical gifts. He wrote songs in imitation of those which he heard, one of which, to his great delight, appeared in the poet's corner of an Aberdeen newspaper. The story which he tells is that on the morning after the poem had been dropped into the mail box, he and a companion waited around the door of the publication office, endeavoring in vain to induce some charitable purchaser to let them have a peep at the contents of the paper, only succeeding at last by crowding the holder of a copy into an entry way and examining the columns by force, being absolutely without the penny with which to buy one. But this success did not stimulate him with any hope of advantage by literature, and he regarded his gift of song writing, like his skill with the flute, as simply the means for his own enjoyment and the amusement of his associates, his ambition shut in within his own little world of squalor and destitution. In appearance he was below the middle stature, and with a club foot, so that physical deformity weighed upon him, as well as the miserable conditions of his life, and made him more sensitive as well as hopeless. For seventeen years he bent over the looms in the School Hill factory, and then removed to the small hamlet of Newtyle, near Dundee, where a cotton factory had been recently established. He now had a family of a wife and four children. In the commercial crash of 1836, after he had been there but a short time, the factory was suspended, only sufficient work being found for the operatives with families to allow them five shillings a week. Five shillings a week for six persons meant starvation and creeping death, " an empty armry and a cold hearthstone." Thom and his family waited week after week, " hoping that times would mend," and with no prospect before them, if they abandoned their miserable pittance, but roadside beggary. He gives the picture of the scene that drove them to the latter alternative.

"Imagine a cold spring forenoon. It is eleven o'clock, but our little dwelling shows none of the signs of that time of day. The four children were still asleep. There is a bed cover hung before the window to keep all within as much like night as possible; and the mother sits beside the beds of her children to lull them back to sleep whenever any one shows an inclination to awake. For this there is a cause, for our weekly five shillings have not come as expected, and the only food in the house consists of a handful of oatmeal saved from the supper of last night. Our fuel is also exhausted.

My wife and I were conversing in sunken whispers about making an attempt to cook the handful of meal, when the youngest child awoke beyond its mother's power to hush it again to sleep, and then fell a-whimpering, and finally broke out in a steady scream, rendering it impossible any longer to keep the rest in a state of unconsciousness. Face after face sprang up, each with one consent exclaiming, 'Oh, mither, mither, gie me a piece.'"

The family took to the road, leaving the key of the miserable tenement with the landlord, in the hope of being eventually able to return to a home like that. By the sale to a pawnbroker in Dundee of "some relics of better days,"—one can hardly imagine what relics or what days,—a small pack of cheap hawker's goods was procured for the wife, and four shillings' worth of books for the husband, to try to sell, but they can only have been the flimsiest disguise for the necessity of depending upon charity. The tramp began, the mother carrying the youngest child on her breast, and often bearing the next youngest also, who was unable to follow the weary road the whole distance. Sunset was followed by cold, sour east winds and rains. At nine o'clock they arrived at a comfortable farm-house, where they were refused shelter, in the absence of the proprietor. All beseeching of the housekeeper was in vain, and the husband returned to the family, who had crept closer together, and were all asleep except the mother.

"Oh, Willie, Willie, what keepit ye. I'm dootfu' o' Jeanie; is na she waesome like? Let's in frae the cauld."

"We've nae wae to gang, lass, whate'er come o' us. Yon folk winnae hae us."

After cowering under a wet mantle in despair for a time, another effort was made. The husband wrote a note by the fast fading light, asking for shelter, and endeavored to have it taken in at a gentleman's mansion near by. It was refused, but a farm laborer was touched by the spectacle of the forlorn family, crouching shelterless in the cold and rain, and took them to a neighboring farmhouse, where they were warmed and fed in the servants' quarters, and put to rest in beds of straw and bagging in an outhouse. Between three and four o'clock the father was wakened by the deadly scream of the mother, who had wakened to find her infant dead by her side, its little life having been worn out by the cold, hunger, and fatigue of the previous day. Amid the wailing of the children, and in the benumbing anguish of the blow, the most vivid remembrance of that moment to the father was the watching of the wheeling and fluttering of a colony of swallows, their fellow-lodgers, who had been awakened by the outcries.

> From perfect grief there need not be
> Wisdom or even memory;
> One thing alone remains to me,
> The woodspurge has a cup of three.

Kind hands assisted in burying the child in the country graveyard, and the tramp was renewed. The poor goods and books would not sell, and no work was to be found, if, indeed, it was more than hopelessly looked for. The people, mostly the poor, "gave bits of bread for the poor bairnies," and shelter was found after nightfall in the out-houses of farms, experience having taught them that it was useless to apply for lodgings during daylight. They met and shared the fortunes of many "gangrel-bodies," some poor and respectable like themselves, and others professional mendicants and wandering ne'er-do-wells to whom beggary was the accustomed mode of livelihood, and many tragedies of life in its last extremity like their own passed under their eyes. One evening, in a gathering of people in the street of the village of Errol, he heard a man of grave countenance and respectable appearance singing, and with that note of despair in his voice which touched his heart with the sympathy like that which made Goldsmith rush from the lighted room to relieve the poor beggar-woman singing under the window. That night in their lodging there was a young woman rocking a corpse-like infant, whose wailing would not be stilled. Then the man who had been singing entered, and bent over the dying child:—

"I have wearied sadly for your coming, James," said the woman.

"It's so dark out by the nicht," replied the man, "I only found out this door by our wean greetin'."

The child died during the night.

At length in the town of Methven, without even the necessary sixpence, preliminary to untieing the shoes in a tramp lodging house, an idea struck Thom that he might make use of his flute to avoid absolute mendicancy. Telling his wife to take the flute from their budget, and to accompany him, he went out into the streets. The story can be told only in his own words.

"We found ourselves in a beautiful green lane, fairly out of town, and opposite a genteel-looking house, at the windows of which sat several well-dressed people. I think that it might be our bewilderment that attracted their notice — perhaps not favorably.

"'A quarter of an hour longer,' said I, 'and it will be darker. Let us walk out a bit.'

"The sun had been down a good while and the gloamin' was lovely. In spite of everything I felt a momentary reprieve. I dipped my dry flute in a little brook and began to play. It rang sweetly amongst the trees. I moved on and on, still playing, and still facing the town. The Flowers of the Forest brought me before the house, lately mentioned. My music raised one window after another, and in less than ten minutes put me in possession of three shillings ninepence of good British money. I sent the mother home with this treasure, and directed her to send the little girl to me. It was by this time nearly dark. Every one says, 'Things just need a beginning.' I have had a beginning and a very good one, too. I had also a turn for strathspeys, and there appeared to be a run on them. By this time I was nearing the middle of the town. When I finally made my way, and retired to my lodging, it was with five shillings and some pence in addition to what was given us. My little girl got a beautiful shawl and some articles of wearing apparel."

He followed up his playing by writing an ode to his flute, which he got printed on slips, and sent in to the houses before which he appeared, with satisfactory results in donations, in one instance receiving the magnificent reward of half a guinea. But, as he says, it was but "beggar's wark," and he was glad to return to his weaving when times got a little better.

After a year at the loom in Aberdeen, he had an

opportunity to work as a journeyman for a weaver, who took in custom work, in the little town of Inverury in the district bordering on Mar. Here, after nine months' residence, his wife, his "faithful Jeanie," died in child-bed, leaving him with three children, the daughter a herd lassie at a lonely farm at some distance. In January, 1841, being then more than forty years of age, and never before having attempted to find a market for his verse, the notion occurred to him, in despair at the dullness of work, to send a poem, entitled The Blind Boy's Pranks, to the Aberdeen Journal. It was prefaced by a note, signed "A Serf," and declaring that the writer was compelled to weave fourteen hours out of the four and twenty. After some time, and while he was engaged in packing the few clothes of himself and children in order to seek shelter at the Aberdeen House of Refuge, he received a letter, with encouraging words, from the editor, and inclosing half a guinea. The poem was widely copied into the Scottish newspapers, and attracted very favorable attention. Among its admirers was a Mr. Gordon of Knockespock, an Aberdeenshire laird, who made inquiries about the author and interested himself in his welfare. It is difficult to understand the sudden and extraordinary popularity of this poem, which is by no means of commanding merit, but the story of

Thom's life became known and he was treated as a literary phenomenon. He was taken on a holiday trip to London by Mr. Gordon, and introduced to the leaders of the Scottish colony there, who made much of him, and on his return he was given a public dinner in Aberdeen. Demands for his verses came upon him from various periodicals, and he was enabled to establish a custom weaving shop in Inverury for himself. The next three years, while he was thus engaged, were the happiest and the only comfortable ones of his life. He refused other offers of employment, and asked no patronage except the purchase of his home-made clothes. He was the head of a little circle of local bards, who looked up to him, and sought his critical approval and patronage for their verses. His fame was increasing and reached a national knowledge in the publication of the volume of his poems, in 1844, by a leading London firm. In an evil hour he was persuaded to give up his business of weaving and establish himself in London as an agent for the sale of weaver's cloth. He was without business knowledge or business habits, lived recklessly and extravagantly, keeping an open house for Chartist agitators and wandering Scottish poets. His inspiration failed him; he wrote little or nothing, and lost his head completely in the whirl of excitement and social dissipation. After three years of this, what he called his "Hospital" was closed by a sheriff's sale of his furniture, and he returned to Scotland by the aid of a subscription from his friends and a grant from the Literary Fund. He settled at Hawkhill, near Dundee, but his health was broken, and his habits of industry destroyed, and he lived recklessly and wretchedly, until death relieved him soon after, in February, 1848. With one fitful gleam of prosperity William Thom's life of half a century had been passed in such want and abject misery as falls to the lot of few mortals, and amid a squalor and degradation of surroundings to which the country poverty of Burns and Hogg, in healthy air and in touch with the sweetness and majesty of nature, was rich and fortunate. One is as surprised and almost shocked to find the flowers of genuine poetry blooming in such a life, as to see a pot of violets growing amid the whirling dust and rattling noise of a weaving factory or in the window of a dingy whiskey shop. That his life was not worse than it was under the influences which affected it, is no less wonderful. "To us," he says, "virtues were known only by their shadows," and that sentence tells all the hopeless misery of an existence in which squalor and unremitting toil were relieved only by the fitful gleams of stupefying indulgence, and in which an ever-pressing want meant the deprivation not only of the comforts, but of the necessities of life. That such a page of human history should be possible and common in the record of a civilized society is more appalling than the devastation of war, or the crimes of natural malignity, and we must wonder how any spark of virtue or genius survived it.

The interest in the life of a man who has written poetry does not make its value. It may add an element of curiosity to biographical history, but it is upon its own inherent quality that it must depend for consideration and remembrance. Extraordinary circumstances in the life and character of the writer may lend an additional interest to his poetry, and cause it to be studied more attentively from a psychological point of view, but it must first be genuine poetry, and the questions of the personality and circumstances of its author are subordinate ones. Other thieves and blackguards like Francis Villon have doubtless written verses in the intervals of their debauches, and other ploughmen like Burns and other weavers like Thom have unquestionably done so under equally difficult and depressing conditions, but that fact has not kept their poetry alive or their names in remembrance. There were contemporaries of Thom, fishermen, turf-cutters, handicraftsmen, and publicans, whose names are preserved in local history and who even published forgotten volumes, who wrote verses under circumstances no less extraordinary than his own, but the world has taken no note of them, and is not called upon to do so. The question in regard to William Thom, as to all other poets, is as to what contribution, small or great, he made to the stock of genuine poetry in form, expression, and essence, fitting it to stand alone and to speak with a living voice to the emotions of the world, aside from any pathos or interest connected with its production. Poetry of this kind in the work of William Thom is very small in quantity. He published but a single volume, in which the verse comprises scarcely more than a hundred pages, and much the greater portion of this is artificial in conception and imperfect in form and expression. Like many uneducated authors, he endeavored to imitate the writers of polite literature, who seemed to him models of taste and fancy, although he had the native good judgment and national feeling to confine himself to the Scottish dialect, and the greater proportion of his verses have this weakness of imitation, or were called forth by special occasions and for a local audience. The poems entitled The Blind Boy's Pranks, which first attracted attention, are fanciful descriptions of the doings of Cupid, who is not more at home on the cold streams and heathery hills of the north of Scotland than on the head of an Italian image seller in the smoke and

grime of London, and has no acquaintance with the
sturdy Scotch lassies with whom he is supposed to
play tricks. The native fairies with which Hogg
peopled the raths and mounds of Ettrick do not
appear in Thom's verses. When he wrote of what
must have appealed most strongly to his heart and
knowledge, the wrongs and sufferings of his fellow
operatives, he was, as has been said, greatly influ-
enced by the perfervid and declamatory style of
Ebenezer Elliot, and weakened the force of his
descriptions by exaggeration and savage invective.
His songs were for the most part in the vein of the
current Scottish lyric poetry, and, although not
without grace and felicity of expression, rarely
above the limits of conventionality and imitation.
The song by which he is most widely known, and
which appears in all the collections of Scottish
poetry, The Mitherless Bairn, owes its vogue to
its simple pathos, appealing to the popular emotions
rather than to its quality as poetry. There are
forcible and felicitous lines scattered through
Thom's poetry, in which the language and melody
combine to render the thought or sentiment with
original power, and touches of description which
show the sensitive eye illumined by the feeling
heart, as this of the winter-beaten birds: —

>   Like beildless birdies, when they ca'
>   Frae wet, wee wing the batted snaw, —

and the pervading genuineness of a deep feeling, even if imperfectly expressed. There was the gloaming of a "waesome light" about his spirit, which shone through his uncertain gifts of utterance, although its power would not have been enough to have preserved his poetry in remembrance, except for two lyrics which reach the very highest level of Scottish song in their completeness and finish of construction, as well as in their simplicity and power. It may be believed from the crudity and imperfection of Thom's other verses that this supreme felicity was accidental, the perfect rapture of some occasional song of a thrush breaking out by its own inspiration after many careless warblings, rather than the deliberate effort of trained skill, and perhaps with little appreciation of their success. Every poet has his moments of supreme success when he reaches beyond his ordinary powers, and execution attains to the level of inspiration, but in most it is seen to be the culmination of trained skill reached by long labor and painstaking effort. There is little, however, in Thom's verse to lead to the expectation of such a flowering of perfect form and expression, and the impression is strong that they are accidental felicities. But, however produced, they give him an indisputable title to a place beside the highest of the Scottish song writers, and will live by their innate grace and power and feeling, when the rest of his work is forgotten, and the record of his strange and unfortunate life swallowed up in oblivion. This is the first one of them, grown from the banks of the Ythan, a little stream near Inverury, where Thom wandered some evening after the day's benumbing labor at the loom: —

YTHANSIDE.

I had ae nicht, and only ane,
    On flow'ry Ythanside;
An' kith or kindred I hae nane
    That dwall by Ythanside;
Yet midnicht dream and morning vow,
    At hame they winna bide,
But pu' and pu' my willing heart
    Awa' to Ythanside.

What gars its restless wand'ring wish
    Seek aye to Ythanside,
An' hover round yon fairy bush
    That spreads o'er Ythanside?
I think I see its pawkie boughs,
    Where lovers weel might hide;
An', oh, what heart could safely sit
    Yon nicht on Ythanside.

Could I return and own the scaith
    I thole frae Ythanside,
Would her mild eye bend lythe on me
    Ance mair on Ythanside?

Or would she crush my lowly love
    Beneath a brow o' pride?
I daurna claim and maurna blame
    Her heart on Ythanside.

I'll rue yon high and heathy seat
    That hangs o'er Ythanside;
I'll rue the mill where burnies meet;
    I'll rue ye, Ythanside.
And you, ye moon, wi' luckless licht,
    Pour'd a' your gowden tide
O'er sic a brow! sic e'en yon nicht!
    Oh, weary Ythanside.

This is the other one in a somewhat different vein, but with equal magic in its melody and tender sweetness of expression:—

WHISPER LOW.

Slowly, slowly the cauld moon creeps
    Wi' a licht unloesome to see;
It dwalls on the window whaur my love sleeps,
    An 'she winna wauken to me.
    Wearie, wearie, the hours, and slow,
    Wauken, my lovie, and whisper low.

There's nae ae sang in heaven's licht,
    Nor on the green earth doun,
Like soun's which kind love kens at nicht,
    When whispers hap the soun';
    Hearin', fearin', sichin' so—
    Whisper, my bonnie love, whisper low!

They lack nae licht wha weel can speak
  In love's ain wordless wile ;
Her ee-bree creepin' on my cheek
  Betrays her pawkie smile.
    Happy, happy, silent so —
    Breathin' bonnie love, whisper low !

Was yon a waft o' her wee white han'
  Wi' a warnin' " wheest " to me ?
Or was it a gleam o' that fause moon fa'in
  On my poor misguided ee ?
    Wearie, wearie, wearie O —
    Wauken, my lovie, an' whisper low !

The poor hand-loom weaver, struggling with the day's darg from the cold dawn to the cheerless night, and with but fitful gleams of light and happiness in the squalid misery of existence, and half unconsciously it may be, has interpreted the sadness and sweetness of love's despair and love's longing, with a melody and a rapture of utterance which touch the immortal sympathies of the heart through the magic of poetry, and will live in the emanations of his spirit to the eyes that for generations to come shall light upon these modest violets of song. Much greater and more fortunate men have failed to join the " choir invisible," and the poetry of loftier and stronger minds has perished, while these songs will remain in the immortal life of simple thought and deep feeling.

FOLK-SONGS OF LOWER BRITTANY.

The publication in 1859 of Count Hersart de Villemarqué's Barzaz Breiz, or collection of ancient Breton ballads and folk-songs, excited almost as much interest in the literary world as Bishop Percy's Reliques of Ancient English Poetry a century earlier, if not reaching to the point of that evoked by Macpherson's Ossian. The interest was historical and ethnological as well as literary. Here were historical ballads, full of fire and passion and pathos, dealing not alone with such comparatively recent and recognized historic figures as Bernard du Guesclin and Jean de Montfort, but dating back to the sixth century and earlier, having for definite characters Merlin and King Arthur, and containing distinct traces of Druidic and bardic influence, which had been preserved, not in manuscript, as were the remains of Celtic poetry in Wales and Ireland, but by oral tradition and as a part of the still living folk-poetry of the people. It was no wonder that great interest was excited by the apparent evidence that a people living in the midst of European civilization had preserved an unbroken tradition of popular poetry for thirteen centuries, with strong traces of heathen influence extending back much farther, in almost absolute purity of language and definite historic characterization, and it was regarded from an ethnologic point of view as of hardly less importance than the discoveries of the remains of the Lake dwellers and other tokens of the existence of prehistoric man. Apparent credibility was given to the authenticity of the collection by the fact that the Breton people had preserved their language in its native condition and form, and by their customs, dress, and manner of life were marked off from the rest of the French people by a distinct line, which showed the strength, originality, and persistence of the race. It was known that they retained the original characteristics of the Celtic race, its fervency of religious faith, its melancholy, its sensitiveness to the mysterious influences of nature, its passion and its loyalty, and that many of its customs and habits of life were distinct survivals of mediævalism, and utterly anomalous to the spirit of modern civilization. It was therefore not thought impossible, if extraordinary, that the ancient ballads should have been preserved in their original purity, and the compositions of the ancient bards and minstrels still remain to be collected from the lips of the wandering mendicant singers, who gathered audiences about them at Fairs and Pardons, or lightened the gloom of the winter evenings in the farm kitchens with song and legend. The character of the ballads in Villemarqué's collection was singularly well adapted to produce this belief. They were simple in construction, impregnated with the characteristics of the people, their faith, their loyalty, their purity and gravity of thought, their subjection to the influence of the supernatural, and their devoted patriotism, and, aside from their genuine strength and elevation as poetry, were a faithful reflection of the thoughts and habits of their people,' and of the authentic facts of their history. There were no signs of such incongruous piecing of the thoughts of a later civilization and the style of a later literature upon an ancient substance, as were visible in Bishop Percy's emendations and completions of the English and Scottish ballads, but they were complete and homogeneous in the very spirit and language of ancient poetry. As a consequence, they were not only accepted as genuine and authentic, but there was an immense interest created in the study and revival of the Breton language and literature, and an appreciation of the characteristics and influence of the Celtic race in France, which has continued and deepened to the present time. An academy was founded, with M. de Villemarqué for its president, and assemblies of bards and scholars were held like the Welsh Eistedfodds, and there was a temporary Breton rage like that for the Highland Scotch under the influence of the Waverley novels, although no ruler of France went so far as to appear in the Breton hat and waistcoat, as George the Fourth did in the Highland kilt during his visit to Edinburgh. Several translations of the ballads of the Barzaz Breiz appeared in German, and Mr. Tom Taylor rendered them into English, in a version singularly compounded of archaic phraseology and stage rhetoric. But the later investigation of careful and conscientious collectors of Breton folk-poetry, like M. F. M. Luzel and others, has destroyed the faith in the authenticity of M. Villemarqué's ballads almost as completely as in that of Macpherson's Ossian. They are not to be found in existence among the present singers or the survivors of the generation from whom M. Villemarqué professed to have gathered them, except in a very mutilated form, and with most of their flowers of poetry ruthlessly swept away. Experiments have been tried at gatherings of the most famous depositories of folk-poetry and the most accomplished singers, by repeating the ballads of the Barzaz Breiz to them, but they have in all cases either professed total ignorance, or insisted upon such amendments as deprived them of all but the faintest resemblance; while the only occasions in which they have been heard sung by the peasantry have been traced to the scattered leaves of the book itself. A hot literary controversy has been waged over the authenticity of M. Villemarqué's ballads, but the best opinion has settled into the belief that they are fabrications and reconstructions from fragments not more authentic and genuine than those which were the basis of Macpherson's Ossian or Chatterton's poems of Rowley, although M. Villemarqué was as thoroughly possessed with the spirit of Breton poetry, and as saturated with the knowledge of Breton history, as Sir Walter Scott was with Scottish poetry and Scottish history, and in one sense they were as genuine as the ballads of The Baron of Smalholme and Thomas the Rhymer. But the idea that the contemporary poems relating to Merlin and King Arthur, and even those of the exploits of Du Guesclin and The Combat of the Thirty, had been preserved in faithful and uncorrupted condition by oral tradition, and were still a portion of the folk-songs of the Breton peasantry, to say nothing of the survival of Druidic poetry and tradition in a distinct form, attractive as it is to the historic imagination, must be given up, like the belief in the survival of the epic of Fingal.

It does not do to expect too much from folk-poetry in the way of the perpetuation of history.

Like the remains of prehistoric people buried in geologic strata, it has been subject to the inevitable destruction of natural forces and to the attrition of time, and only remains like the fragments of implements and the piles of kitchen middens, from which careful study can extract the evidences of former existence and habits. It is only when ancient poetry has been committed to writing, like the poems of Homer and the Scandinavian sagas, that it can be preserved in anything like a complete state; and while there is a singular tenacity in popular poetry, it cannot endure for centuries by oral tradition alone, however secluded the people or however strong their national and poetic spirit. Sir Walter Scott was only just in time to save the Border ballads of the previous two centuries, and the usual duration of popular ballads in anything but an indistinct and fragmentary condition is even less. But, although the authenticity of the ballads of the Barzaz Breiz is discredited, it cannot be said that there is no genuine and valuable Breton folk-song. On the contrary, it exists in very great quantity and of a high quality, not only as poetry, but as illustrating the character and history of the people. The Breton race is not only a profoundly poetical one, by its pensive, mystic, and deeply religious character, but by its secluded condition apart from the currents of modern education, and its occupations in the gloomy, wind-swept, and rain-beaten fields and on the mysterious and terrifying seas, is particularly subject to the influences which make folk-song a part of its life and the natural expression of its thoughts and emotions. Nor is its folk-poetry entirely without value in the strictly historical sense, although anything like absolute accuracy or the definite remains of contemporary historic verse are not to be expected. As in the extant folk-lore of other nations, the roots run far back, and evidences of the traditions and customs of former ages survive in a fragmentary and altered state, in which may be traced the tokens of the existence of the race in the earliest dawn of history and even before any known records. Thus, if there are no authentic poems of the time of Merlin and King Arthur in the Breton folk-songs of the present day, their names and traditions survive; and, if the school culture of the Druids does not survive in the poems of numeral questions on the characters and events of the Bible, as imagined or invented by M. Villemarqué, no less fragments of their customs and worship remain in the habits and traditions of the people in and outside of their religious ritual, and are perpetuated in their folk-songs, if with as little definite knowledge as of the rites once performed at the feet of the dolmens or in the temple of Karnac. The fairies, and the dwarfs, and the spirits of the sea and air still survive, and are dreaded or invoked in the same spirit, if with less fervency than the saints and powers of the Church. Thus M. Paul Sebillot, in his Contes des Marins, gathered in Upper Brittany, tells that the sailors shake their fists at and threaten with their knives an unfavorable wind, and there are numerous actual customs as well as traditions among the Breton people which are evident survivals from heathen ages, while the rites of the Church itself have many traces of the adoption of forms of nature worship. This element of the supernatural, like the traditions of actual history, is fading away in Brittany as in all other countries, but enough remains to throw a strong light on the ancient customs, as well as the fundamental character of the race, and to inform its folk-poetry with this element to a degree which that of few modern nations possesses.

The interest of modern folk-poetry is, however, mainly in quality as poetry, its expression with eloquence and feeling of the emotions of the human heart, and the representation which it gives of the quality of the mind, the temperament, the degree of intelligence, and the habits and customs of the people who produced it. In this view the two latest volumes of the collection of Breton folk-songs by F. M. Luzel, Sonniou Breiz-Izel (Paris,

Emile Bouillon, 1890), are particularly interesting. His two previous volumes, Gwerzion Breiz-Izel, were devoted to the fantastic, supernatural, and tragic ballads which held a place by the side of the fabulous tales in the minds of the people, were derived from the remote past, and had little connection with the life of to-day. On the contrary, the Sonniou, for which songs is the somewhat imperfect equivalent in English, are the immediate interpretation of their thoughts and emotions, the transcripts of their present life, and its events, sung and told by living poets, or those who have lived within a time to make them a part of the present people. They include the songs which are sung by the cradles to drowsing infants, the hopes and sorrows of love, the joyous welcomes to weddings, the homely pains of married life, and the sorrows for the common lot of death, the chants of religious faith and worship, the charms against diseases, the accompaniments of labor and the peculiarities of trade and occupation, the homely reflections on the conduct of life, and the rustic humor and satire, and, in short, all the thoughts and events, which mark the daily life of the people. Of their absolute genuineness there can be no question. They have all the internal evidence in their construction and language, the simplicity and abruptness of thought, the imperfection of utterance combined with untaught eloquence and strength, the occasional vulgarity by the side of an equally great delicacy, the simple and powerful melody, and all the characteristics of popular poetry, which are as unmistakable as the perfumes of the flowers of the field. Their collection has been the work of forty-five years, in which M. Luzel has indefatigably traversed the provinces of Lower Brittany, visiting the solitary huts of the sabot makers and hemp-weavers, colloquing with wandering beggars, listening to the songs and stories at the kitchen firesides of lonely farms in winter, gathering the singers at the Fair around him in the tap-rooms, taking down the songs of nursing mothers, the sailors on shipboard and the soldiers in the barracks, the shepherds on the plains and the laborers in the fields, and, in short, gathering every form of verse which is the expression of the popular thoughts and emotions. They are naturally of less purely literary merit than the ballads of the Barzaz Breiz, which are carefully arranged, trimmed, and decorated for poetical effect. It is always a sign for suspicion when folk-poetry is too good. The picturesque garments of the Breton peasantry must show the signs of actual wear and even the stains of grease and dirt, if they are to have the genuine effect, and when they are of too fine material, too carefully arranged, and shining and spotless, the impression is that they are simply stage costumes drawn from the theatrical wardrobe. Even the beggar with his rags too artistically draped suggests the painter's model. So there must be the element of reality in their defects before the folk-songs can be accepted as really genuine, and it adds a power and even a literary effect to them, which in its peculiar flavor the most accomplished literary art cannot produce. We seem to hear the speech of living men, to feel the thoughts of simple hearts through the imperfect utterance, and to experience all the flavor of actual and homely life. The pieces in the Sonniou collected by M. Luzel have all this quality. They have the coarse material and the patches of garments actually worn, and their charm is due to their native picturesqueness and originality. There is no false sentiment, however deep the feeling, and the homely thoughts are expressed in homely phrases, with natural imagery drawn from the aspect of nature about them and their avocations in life. Their standard of conventionality in speech differs from that of polite society, and there are words and phrases which smack of a coarse and natural life, but they are, nevertheless, singularly pure in thought, and show the soundness and honesty of the Breton character, as well as its tenderness and warmth of affection. If not great refinement, there is great depth of feeling, and actual vulgarity of thought is as rare as immoral suggestion, even in the rude satires and humorous narratives.

The beginning of all folk-song is in the cooing melodies which the mothers chant by the inspiration of nature by the cradles of their drowsing infants, and in which the affections of their hearts take an articulate form as naturally as the songs of birds. The *berceuses*, or cradle songs, of the Breton peasantry have all the elements of deep feeling and childish simplicity of expression which characterize the voice of motherhood in every clime and every station in life, and unite the queen and the peasant in a common bond. The same lovely and touching images suggest themselves, and the same simple and soothing melody flows naturally from the lips. This Breton cradle song might find its parallel in thought and language in many nations : —

CRADLE SONG.

Toutouie la, la, my little child,
Toutouie la, la.

Your mother is here, my little child,
To rock you softly, little dear.

Your mother is here, my little lamb,
She will sing you a little song.

The other day she wept sorely ;
Now she smiles, the little mother.

Toutouie la, la, my little bird,
In the sweet breast of thy rose tree.

To fly to heaven, my little angel,
Do not spread your little wing.

There is also the element of infantile humor, as in all nursery songs, to bring smiles to the rosy cheeks, with food for the simple imagination opening its eyes on the birds and beasts around it, and endowing them with human life. One can feel how a child would appreciate the little story of The Fox Gallant with a sense at once of reality and humor: —

THE FOX GALLANT.

I had a pullet and I had but one,
A fox carried her off, and now I have none.

The fox has carried her off from the sill of my door,
And more than that, I think, he has done me disgrace.

But I perceive Jean le Ri and also Herod,
And I ask them, have you not seen my pullet.

And I pass my head out of the front room window.
I see my pullet, who on the village green is dancing,

And the fox by her side with a Flanders basket;
With pears and with apples he is treating my pullet.

Next to cradle songs, the creations of motherly affection, come the songs of youthful passion, when the instinct of love wakes in the hearts of the young man and the maid; and they sing, also, as naturally and simply as birds do in pairing time. There is often a touching inconsequence in these simple strains, a transcript of nature as it speaks to the heart, and finds almost inarticulate utterance in emotions of joy and sorrow, which is like the warbling of a bird, often ending its trill of gladness with a plaintive note. And the verses entitled The Song of the Nightingale, with its inconsequent but natural imageries at the close, which has an effect beyond the reach of art, has this penetrating and realistic effect: —

THE SONG OF THE NIGHTINGALE.

Sing, sing, nightingale, it is early you are singing.
Not earlier than you, young man. Hunting are you going?
Good luck to you, little comrade. I am not going a-hunting.
I am on my way to Kerlosquet, where my love is dwelling.
The nightingale then asked him, being a curious gossip,
There are many houses at Kerlosquet, to which one are you going?
The young man answered her in a tone of humor,
Good luck to you, little comrade, I am not at confession.
In a moment after he saw his mistress coming;
By her color and her looks he saw that she was ailing.
Anxiously he asked her, feeling for her sadness,
Are you sick at heart, or sick in your spirit?
And she answered, with a little smile so gracious,

I am not subject to sickness, no, by the mercy of Jesus.
— The spider does well to spin his web,
To spin and to spread it and to dry it on the meadow.
A breath of wind will come and bear it away.
The hearts of young men are like it.

The most numerous producers of love songs in the Breton folk-poetry are the *cloer*, or young theological students, to whose title the English word clerk, as it was understood in the time of Chaucer, is the nearest equivalent. These young men, mostly the sons of peasants or persons in humble circumstances, are destined for the priesthood, for which they have manifested a vocation by their special intellectual brightness or devotional temperament. They are naturally the pride and hope of their families, to whom the office of priest is a position of worldly advancement and religious reverence, and the ballads tell touching tales of sacrifices by poor parents to enable their son to pursue his studies. They are sent to the seminaries attached to the abbeys in the various cathedral towns, from which they return in the vacation to mingle with the life of the people. Although destined for the priesthood, the instinct of youthful passion breaks out, as they meet the young maidens of the neighborhood in the fields or at the village fêtes and gatherings, and there are struggles of love and longing, which sometimes end peacefully in the surrender of the affection to the demands of the priestly vow, sometimes in the tragedy of broken hearts and a double devotion to religious celibacy, and sometimes, under the influence of a stronger passion, in the renunciation of the priesthood and marriage with the object of affection. These young clerks are, naturally, objects of great attraction to the young maidens by the contrast of their superior manners and education to the duller and coarser young men of the peasant class, and this attraction results in many dramas of love, not to mention the deeper tragedies of blighted passions and ruined lives. From their superior intellectual activity and education the young clerks are the most fertile and eloquent of the folk-poets, and by far the greater number of the love songs in the Sonniou are their production, and relate to the condition in which their affections are bound and limited. Their songs are genuine folk-poetry in their simplicity and strength of expression, except in the few instances where sophomoric pedantry overloads them with mythologic terms and academic phrases, and they often express a deep feeling with simple and natural eloquence. In The Ditty of Love the young girl appeals to the clerk to abandon the priesthood, since there are enough priests in the country, and expect the blessing of God in marrying the one who loves him, and then resigns herself to the consolation they will have in hearing the bells of each other's convents and their voices raised in psalm: —

THE DITTY OF LOVE.

When from my books I turn to the sight of the world,
I am touched by a prick, which troubles my spirit.

I fancy I hear the sweet voice of my mistress
Speak with a tone that is melting with sadness.

Whenever my mistress raises her voice in song,
The fairies of the mountain reëcho the air.

The fishes in the sea dart about rejoicing,
And the sailors on the deck dance gaily as they hear it.

The rocks upon the mountain split themselves asunder
In hearing her voice and seeing her beauty.

When I cast a glance, which rests upon my mistress,
It seems to me I see the queen of all the maidens.

Her dainty hands are mingled with red and with white,
And her eyes are brilliant as the stars in the sky.

Her two cheeks are roses of a natural color,
And her lips are as sweet as the pure honeycomb.

— Good morning, my fair maiden, on my knees I fall
To ask your benediction to become a Capuchin.

To ask your benediction to become a Recollet,
In St. Francis convent, in the village of Morlaix.

— Oh, enough of Recollets has St. Francis's convent,
And enough of priests has the village of Morlaix.

There are enough of priests everywhere in the country,
Marry the one you love, and God will also love you.

If you become a Recollet at St. Francis convent,
I will go to the Calvary and there become a nun.

There we will hear together the bells of our two convents,
And there we will be singing the praises of our Lord.

There we will be singing, with our lifted voices,
The *Gloria in Excelsis* and the *Salve Regina*.

The hero of the piece entitled I will be neither Priest nor Monk is made of more determined stuff, and demands that his books shall be thrown into the fire, and liberty given him to marry the object of his love, or else he will die: —

I WILL BE NEITHER PRIEST NOR MONK.

Between the prairie and the grassy hill,
There is a bridge, I know it to my will.

No one can pass at eve along its planks,
Because of scholars rude, who play their pranks.

When at prayers I should be at grand mass,
No pater nor ave from my lips does pass.

Across my shoulder I only fix my glance
On the young girl, who causes my mischance.

I see my sweet beneath the shadowed nave,
As the lily fair, and as the red gold brave.

A cambric cap upon her head sets well,
Which cost, at least, six ecus for an ell.

And underneath a fine coiffure of lace,
That like a lily's margin frames her face.

Her petticoat, so rounded and so gay,
Shines with a double silver cord's display.

A robe she wears as red as any coal,
And, oh, I love her in my inmost soul.

— Put money in your pocket, little fool,
And to Treguier take your way to school.

Go to Treguier, and there study well,
Become a priest and follow the church bell.

— Keep your money in your own purse for me,
For, by my faith, no priest nor monk I'll be.

My books throw in the fire, and let them burn,
Or give them to my brother in his turn.

No priest or monk I ever shall be made,
My heart demands the love of a fair maid.

A lovely maid of Cornouaille, I ween,
With eyes of blue and locks of amber sheen.

And if I cannot have that golden head,
Prepare the mass, for soon I shall be dead.

In The Secrets of the Clerk there is a more delicate fancy, and the gracious avowal has all the charm of a natural and touching imagery: —

THE SECRETS OF THE CLERK.

Each night, each night, as on my bed I lie,
I do not sleep, but turn myself and cry.

I do not sleep, but turn myself and weep,
When I think of her I love so deep.

Each day I seek the Wood of Love so dear,
In hopes to see you at its streamlet clear.

When I see you come through the forest grove,
On its leaves I write the secrets of my love.

— But a fragile trust are the forest leaves,
To hold the secrets close which their page receives.

When comes the storm of rain, and gusty air,
Your secrets close are scattered everywhere.

'T were safer far, young clerk, on my heart to write.
Graven deep they'd rest, and never take their flight.

The amatory folk-songs of Brittany have their peculiar images and phrases, like those of all other countries, and which are repeated without variation as almost essential characteristics. The reader of Scottish ballads knows how invariably the recipient of a letter first smiles and then has his eyes blinded by tears, and recalls the constant repetition of familiar images and descriptions. So in the Breton folk-songs the lover constantly declares that he has worn out three pairs of sabots in coming to see her without being able to find out her thought, and that he has watched in the wind and rain through the night with no consolation but the sound of her soft breathing through the key-hole of the door; to which the cruel or coquettish damsel replies that she has no objection to tell him her thought, which is that he should buy a new pair of shoes, or that he should take himself home as soon as possible. The piece entitled In the White Cabin at the Foot of the Mountain is a characteristic specimen of these songs, whose effect of simplicity can only be retained by an absolutely literal translation:—

> In the white cabin at the foot of the mountain
> Is my sweet, my love.
>
> Is my love, is my desire,
> And all my happiness.
>
> Before the night I must see her
> Or my little heart will break.
>
> My little heart will not break
> For my lovely dear I have seen.
>
> Fifty night I have been
> At the threshold of her door; she did not know it.

The rain and the wind whipped me,
Until my garments dripped.

Nothing came to console me
Except the sound of breathing from her bed.

Except the sound of breathing from her bed,
Which came through the little hole for the key.

Three pairs of shoes I have worn out,
Her thought I do not know.

The fourth pair I have begun to wear,
Her thought I do not know.

Five pairs, alas, in good count,
Her thought I do not know.

— If it is my thought you wish to know,
It is not I, who will make a mystery of it.

There are three roads on each side of my house,
Choose one among them.

Choose whichever you like among them,
Provided it will take you far from here.

— More is worth love, since it pleases me,
Than wealth with which I do not know what to do.

Wealth comes, and wealth it goes away,
Wealth serves for nothing.

Wealth passes like the yellow pears :
Love endures for ever.

More is worth a handful of love
Than an oven full of gold and silver.

Another form of the love song than the melancholy apostrophe to the mistress, and the simple moralizing which accompanies it, is the gay chant, which was composed to the dance measures played by the *biniou* and the *bombarde* at the village fêtes, and which was sung in accord with them. On these occasions, which were chiefly the Pardons, or gatherings to celebrate the days of the Patron Saints, when the religious exercises are concluded, the young men engage in athletic competition, wrestling and jumping for prizes under the eyes of their sweethearts, and the festivities wind up with dancing on the green, and the scene is as gay as if it had no connection with religion. Every Breton story teller, and every writer on the life and customs of Brittany, has delighted to depict these scenes, which are the rendezvous of youthful lovers and the embodiment of vigorous and healthy gayety, with all the picturesqueness of country life and color. The element of these dance songs is their lively and strongly accented melody to accompany the dancing air and illustrate the movements, as in the following specimen : —

> Sunday I have seen,
>   Sunday I will see,
> Three of my young lovers,
>   Who'll come and dance with me.

Dance between the two,
    And pass before them gay,
Dance between the three,
    And wave them all away.

Press the foot of that;
    And wink the eye at this;
Mock the other's pride;
    There is no greater bliss.

When you come to call,
    Pray let me know the hour;
I will grease my cakes
    And put eggs in the flour.

I will oil the door;
    The hinges will not creak;
In the closet bed
    I'll lie, and will not speak.

Come not through the yard,
    My flowers you will tread,
My onions, and my cress,
    My peas and berries red.
Throw straw upon the fire
    To show your darling head.

It might be expected that in a country so much under the influence of the sea, and in which so large a proportion of the inhabitants are sailors, fishers on the stormy and dangerous coast or in the distant waters of Newfoundland and Iceland, there would be a large number of sea songs. The folk-lore of Brittany is particularly rich in stories and legends of the sea, composed by the fishermen to while away the long hours of the passage to Newfoundland or the nightwatches in the misty seas of Iceland; or embodying the mysterious and superstitious terrors of the fishermen of the coast in the face of storms and foaming reefs; and the impress of supernatural power in the ocean and the storm is very strong upon the imaginations of the Breton people. But the sailors themselves, like the laborers in the fields, do not seem to have the inspiration and poetical gift to put their thoughts into song. M. Luzel has been able to collect but a comparatively few of genuine sailor songs, and these are mostly tavern choruses or rude and commonplace chants, with but very little of the salt of the seas and the voice of the breeze in them. The women sometimes chant at the spinning-wheel songs of warning against the dangers and perils of becoming a sailor's wife, of which the following is an example: —

DO NOT MARRY A SAILOR.

Maidens young, who wish to wed,
Take advice from an old head.

If you marry, as you say,
Do not take a sailor gay.

If you take a sailor gay,
You will sorrow night and day.

When the farmer's wife's in bed
The sailor's wife the floor must tread.

When the wind arises shrill,
Her heart will beat, her eyes will fill.

Her heart will beat, her eyes will fill,
And in her veins the blood run chill.

Every moment she seeks the door,
— Mercy, how the torrents pour!

If I had store of money red,
I know the husband I would wed.

I'd wed the heir of a good house,
Who can reap the fields he ploughs.

Who can reap the fields he ploughs,
And in his stable has good cows.

Both night and day whom I can see,
And who will sleep by the side of me.

While the poor sailor, day and night,
Lives in peril and affright.

Day and night must work and wake,
And of a plank his cradle make.

The Breton women, who spend hours at the spinning-wheel, as in all other countries, accompany the monotonous and musical drone with long chants, that hypnotize the sense of labor, which are often merely improvisations with as little sense and meaning as the lullabies for infants. But here is one into which the old spinner puts the thoughts of her willingness to make sacrifice of her all in order that her son might be educated as a priest, and her hopes of reward from his filial piety. The soothing and monotonous melody is necessarily lost in the translation.

THE SONG OF THE OLD SPINNER.

My wheel and my bonnet of straw
And my waist of white linen

Shall be all yours, my young clerk,
That you may make yourself a priest.

And my porringers and my spoons,
He shall have them all at one time.

And my old warp, and my brake,
And my old carder besides.

And when he is a priest
I shall have a broidered robe.

And my shoes will have ribbons,
And my collar will be fluted.

And a cap upon my head,
Like that of a damsel of quality.

One of the most notable and singular features in Breton folk-poetry is the feeling displayed toward animals. Almost human attributes of wisdom and affection are bestowed upon them, and, unlike many primitive races, the Breton peasantry have a great tenderness toward the dumb companions of their labors. When they kill them it is from necessity, and with a genuine sensibility for their sufferings, which may have its ancient root in a tradition of animal worship, such as led the North American Indian to apologize to the bear, whom he was killing with his arrows. At any rate it is a very creditable feeling, and adds to the respect and liking which the Breton character inspires, that there should be this tenderness for the old horse, who has ploughed the fields and borne burdens until his strength is spent; for the old goat, who has given milk for the children; and even for the pig, who has inhabited the pen by the cabin. In the folk-songs this feeling is represented by various pieces of verse, giving the last wills and testaments of old animals, who bequeath, sometimes in a spirit of humor, and sometimes with affectionate tenderness, portions of their bodies and qualities of their spirits to their human friends and companions. There is thus the testament of the goat, the old sow, and the old mare. The latter displays a touching feeling, and the impression of quaint absurdity gives way to a more tender emotion and that touch of pathos which is evoked by all animal affection and animal suffering.

THE WILL OF THE OLD MARE.

Between Pontrieaux and Kerlouet
Is dead an old mare.

She cried, the old mare,
To have her shoes pulled off.

She cried loud enough to split her voice,
— Pull the nails from my sabots.

It is eighteen months, without falsehood,
Since I have been in a stable.

If it is not in the great barnyard of Kerlouet,
There I have often lodged.

I bequeath my patience
To him, Oliver le Judic.

Which he has cruelly proved this year,
In that he has lost his wife.

In that this year his wife is dead.
To live without one's half is not a pleasant thing.

I pray to give the hairs of my tail,
To him, Pierre l'errot.

That he may make a light fly-flap
To keep the flies from the horses in summer.

And when the other horses fling and kick,
He will remember the blind mare.

Carry my head to the ferry of Frinaoudour,
To serve as a little boat upon the water.

To pass from one bank to the other
Those who go to hunt at Plourivo.

Those who go to hunt at Plourivo,
The rabbit, the fox and the wild duck.

As has been said, the chief value of folk-song is in its genuineness, in the accuracy with which it reflects not only the emotions, but the habits and customs of the people, so that their peculiar life becomes visible before our eyes. There is an indefinable charm, not only in the impression of reality, but in the very rudeness and imperfection of the speech, which gives an effect beyond literary art, when deep emotion or domestic pathos are seen through it. We seem to get nearer the primitive heart of mankind than under the effect of the most accomplished literary skill, and there are awakened the homely and tender feelings which lie deep within our nature. The genuine fairy tale created by the vivid and credulous imagination of the uncultivated mind, and the genuine folk-song, the outburst of simple and natural emotion, take a hold upon even the most cultivated intellects as the highest literary art fails to do. The folk-songs of Brittany have this charm as well as their own peculiar provincial flavor; and the very crudeness and imperfection of the Sonniou in M. Luzel's collection have more power than all the elaborate poetry and picturesqueness of M. Villemarqué's Celtic fabrications.

THE FOLK-SONGS OF POITOU.

WHILE there is much that is common in the folk-songs of all the provinces of France, the same stories and the same turns of expression, showing, if not a common origin, a very wide and thorough intercommunication, — as, for instance, in the beautiful and pathetic ballad of Jean Renaud, which is found almost everywhere in slightly differing variants, — each section has its own local peculiarities illustrating the temperament and the origin of the people. It is needless to say that there is a strongly marked note of difference between the melancholy and finely sensitive songs of the people of Brittany and the gay and joyous chants and ballads of those of Gascony and Provence. It would be inevitable from the widely different natures of the two people, and their origin from distinct and strongly divergent native stocks. But this distinction goes further, and marked shades of difference in feeling and sentiment may be found in the character and temperament of the folk-songs and music of the inhabitants of the same province, who are of common origin and consanguinity, with the same native language, and the same habits and customs. This is due in a great measure to a difference in their surroundings, and the influence of external nature, whether gay or morose, fertile or barren, upon the minds and characters of the people. Thus in his splendid collection of the Chants and Chansons Populaires des Provinces de l'Ouest, M. Jerome Burgeaud tells us that the plaintive and melancholy airs of the inhabitants of the deep woods and heavy marshes of La Vendee become gay and cheerful in Poitou, and sparkle with brilliant mirth in Saintonge and the Angumois, without changing their notes or form, simply from the difference in the scenery and its influence upon the spirits of the people. The ancient Poitou, comprising the upper portion of the region between the Loire and Garonne, is full of smiling and rich fields, where the grapes burgeon in deep black clusters, and the yellow wheat-ears hang heavy and full, and the warm sun and the savory air fill the blood of the people with lightness and gayety. They are not so ebullient and joyous, it may be, as the inhabitants of the still warmer and more smiling regions of Gascony and Languedoc, but the contrast is very marked between them and their northern neighbors, whose very mirth has a melancholy tinge, and in whom even drunkenness is a protest against sorrow rather than the natural extravagance of light-heartedness.

The Poitevin peasant is naturally gay, and his light-heartedness is manifested in the great number, as well as in the good humor and cheerfulness, of his folk-songs. Of course the common sorrows of mankind weigh upon him; he feels the stings of poverty and the pains and sordidness of labor; the conscription tears him from his home and his beloved; and he experiences the tragedies of love and death. These things stir his mind and find a place in his folk-songs, but the prevailing spirit which governs his expression in music and song is not of melancholy brooding and sorrow, like that of his Celtic neighbors, but gayety and joyousness. He finds the smiling world a pleasant place to live in; his love is the natural and happy ebullition of his warm temperament; and his experiences of life are cheerful.

The gayety of the Poitevin temperament finds its expression in the immense number of "rounds" as they are called in English, which give the vocal measure and accompaniment to the vigorous and joyous dances. The youths and the maidens, when they meet at the rustic gatherings, or even in the intervals of labor in the fields, join hands by a natural instinct, and improvise a dance to the rhythm of their own voices, and the "rounds" which they sing, although often mere nonsense, or at least without a consecutive meaning, have a note of gayety and an ebullition of joyousness, which is inimitable, as thus:—

> Vous, qui menez la ronde,
> Menez la rondement.
>
> Son cotillon en branle, en branle,
> Son cotillon en branle au vent.
>
> Foule, foule, foulons l'herbe,
> L'herbe foule reviendra.
>
> Brunette, allons, gai, gai, gai,
> Brunette, allons, gai, gaiment.

— words which interpret the air and accent the steps with an absolute perfection, which a translation cannot render, although it may give an idea of the vivacity and *entrain*.

> You, who lead the round,
> Lead it roundily.
>
> Her petticoat in motion, in motion,
> Her petticoat in motion to the wind.
>
> Tread, tread, come tread the grass,
> The trodden grass will spring again
>
> Brunette, come, gay, gay, gay,
> Brunette, come, gay, gaily.

All these, like the ancient choruses with which the Greek maidens accompanied their dances of "woven paces and waving hands," with or without the note of a primitive reed to accent the melody, are reproduced in the grosser spirit of the laboring peasant, but equally instinctive with life and gayety, and the natural expression of youthful existence in the open air and under balmy skies.

One of the most characteristic features of the Poitevin peasant is his cunning, his fondness for rustic ruses, and the sharp repartee or trick, which puts to shame the person of a station above his own. The heroines of many of his favorite ballads and songs are endowed with this quality, and he chuckles with a hearty zest at the simple wit with which the shrewd shepherdess puts down the amorous gallant learned in the schools, or escapes the dangerous importunity of a gentleman on the highway or a seignorial hunter in the fields. The folk-songs of Poitou are full of such examples, and M. Bugeaud, and M. Leon Pineau, who has followed him in gleaning in the same field (Le Folk-Lore du Poitou), have given a number of specimens. The following shows what simple repartee appeals to the rustic sense of humor: —

NANON.

What is there, Nanon,
 In these valleys green?
There is a fool, kind sir,
 When you are therein.

Pray tell me, Nanon,
    Where does this road go?
When you have found out,
    Then you will know.

Come, my dear Nanon,
    Under the green shade.
Would you have me think
    Of heat you're afraid?

Is he then happy,
    The shepherd you know?
If he is unhappy,
    He does n't seem so.

You love him, Nanon,
    As I adore you?
Yes, indeed, kind sir,
    And much better too.

Pray tell me, Nanon,
    Who made you so smart?
You, too, have studied,
    And learned things by heart.

In my father's house,
    I have studied deep.—
I got my learning
    In watching my sheep.

One of the favorite ruses is that by which the shepherd maid induces the gallant to let her go, on some frivolous excuse and a promise to return, and then mocks him for his credulity. A similar jest, with the proverb that when you hold a quail in hand you should pluck it, is very common in French folk-song, as, indeed, in that of all nations. This is one of the Poitevin versions : —

THE SHEPHERDESS AND THE GENTLEMAN.

It was a gentleman returning from the army,
   Upon the road he met a shepherd maid ;
He dismounted quickly, and went to sit beside her.
   Cunning was the maid, and wept as if afraid.

"Have mercy, gentleman, you 'll spoil my fine, white cap,
   I 'll go and put it off, and come back quite soon."
The gallant gentleman found the time quite tedious,
   The maiden did not come ; he whistled a blank tune.

"John, my little John, go and tell the maiden
   To come back at once, for she must be asleep."
"Good fortune it is to me that I have got away,
   By the grace of God I have no shame to weep."

"Little John returned to where his master waited,
   Whistling a blank tune beneath the willow tree,
"Alas, my master, the maid is very cunning ;
   She is safe at home, and sends you mockery."

The gallant ceased his tune, and swore in bitter anger,
   "If again that maid I meet by any hap,
Either in the highroad, or on the flowery meadow,
   I will have no mercy on her fine, white cap."

Then the love songs of Poitou have a light and humorous turn, a jest at the fickleness of the run-away lover, and the easy consolation of the young maiden, whose desire is more to have a lover than that he should be any particular person. La Belle Rosalie illustrates this gay mockery of youthful love.

THE FAIR ROSALIE.

The fair Rosalie
   Has lost her lover bold,
Is n't she unhappy,
   Only fifteen years old!

He promised to return, —
   The deep woods were to blame, —
But she has waited vainly;
   The traitor never came.

"Nightingale that sings,
   Nightingale that flies,
Tell me, tell me truly,
   Where my lover lies."

"Your lover, maiden fair,
   Has gone across the Rhine.
Captains three are with him,
   And he is brave and fine.

"Exchange your woman's dress
   For a soldier's coat of blue:

"In thirty days you 'll find him,
    If you his route pursue."

When she arrived at Bruges,
    She found her lover there,
Training with the soldiers,
    With banners floating fair.

"If I had known, my dear,
    You would have followed me,
You would not have found me,
    For I 'd have crossed the sea."

"Am I not unhappy,
    To march so far to find
The traitor, whom I love,
    And who is so unkind ?

"Nightingale that sings,
    And who hast flown so far,
Tell me, tell me truly,
    Where other lovers are."

But all the other lads
    Have sought for other brides,
And taken for their spouses
    The sabres at their sides.

The Veille des Noces gayly mocks the impatience of the young maiden for the dawn of her wedding day, which will not allow her to rest quiet in bed, or endure without reply the rebuke of her more contented mother : —

THE NIGHT BEFORE MY WEDDING.

The night before my wedding,
  Guess what happened me.
I rose up to the window,
  If daybreak I could see —
    The dawn of day,
    The lovely dawn of day,
    Of light and love so gay.

I rose up to my window,
  If daybreak I could see,
The lovely moon still shining
  Was all that greeted me.

The lovely moon still shining,
  Was all the sign of light.
I thought it must be four o'clock,
  But 't was not yet midnight.

I thought it must be four o'clock,
  But midnight had not sped.
My mother, who was listening,
  Heard the cross words I said.

My mother, who was listening,
  Heard the sad sighs I drew.
" Be silent, little fool," she said,
  " Or God will punish you !

" Be silent, little fool," she said,
  Or God will bring you loss."

"O, mother dear, do you not know
    What 't is that makes me cross?

"O, mother dear, do you not know,
    What 't is that gives me pain,
You lie at ease, but I do not;
    I must get up again."

There is also a flavor of mockery in the naïve dialogue between the shepherd, Joseph, and his mistress, whom he has come to waken in the morning, and to invite to spend the day with him on the mountain. The shepherdess wants to be assured of something more substantial than mere affection before she yields to the temptation.

JOSEPH.

Joseph, your faithful shepherd,
    Has come to waken you,
Arise, my lovely maiden,
    My lovely maiden, rise —
The sun shines bright and new.

Alas, my faithful shepherd,
    Whither shall we go?
Above, upon the mountains
    Where shining streamlets flow,
Where we will gather violets,
    And rosemary also.

Alas, my faithful shepherd,
    What shall be our food?

> A pie of tender larks,
>   And cakes so sweet and good,
> And see, beneath my mantle
>   A flask of grapes' rich blood.
>
> Alas, my faithful shepherd,
>   In what place shall we sleep?
> Above, in my thatched cottage,
>   Within the wood so deep.
> I have a place of shelter
>   Wherein no cold can creep.
>
> Alas, my faithful shepherd,
>   What if my father knew?
> Tell him, my beloved,
>   That your shepherd true
> Came upon the mountain
>   To keep the wolf from you.

In Le Berger qui me fait le Cour, the shepherdess displays more grace and sentiment in refusing to point out the identity of her lover, while avowing her charming and spontaneous affection.

THE SHEPHERD WHO MAKES LOVE TO ME.

> The shepherd who makes love to me,
> The shepherd who makes love to me,
> Is the bravest you can see.
> Ask me not to tell you more.
>
> I lead my sheep upon the plain,
> I lead my sheep upon the plain,

And my cows to browse again.
Ask me not to tell you more.

My lambkins feed along the glade,
My lambkins feed along the glade,
And I am seated in the shade.
Ask me not to tell you more.

My shepherd comes to see me there,
My shepherd comes to see me there,
And tells me I am sweet and fair.
Ask me not to tell you more.

In listening to his love words deep,
In listening to his love words deep,
My eyelids close ; I'm charmed to sleep.
Ask me not to tell you more.

I dream my shepherd is a dove,
I dream my shepherd is a dove,
And my fond heart his cage of love,
Ask me not to tell you more.

The maiden surprised by her lover as she lies asleep beneath the shade is a favorite subject in all folk-poetry, but it is seldom that it has been treated with a greater grace and charm than in La Belle Endormie. The sentiment has all the simplicity and purity of spontaneous love, and the language the sweet naïveté of folk-song, however much of its charm may have vanished in the translation.

THE FAIR ONE ASLEEP.

In walking in the garden,
   To shun the burning light,
I saw beneath the leafage
   A maid of beauty bright.
With noiseless feet I crept
To where the damsel slept.

With noiseless feet I tip-toed
   To give her no alarm,
Her head had for a pillow
   Her round and rosy arm,
As softly as the air
I kissed her dreaming there.

And while she lay in slumber,
   I sought a garden bed,
And on her snowy bosom
   I placed a rosebud red.
The flower's breath of balm
Dispelled her slumber's charm.

When slumber's charm had vanished,
   She woke with laughing eyes;
Oh, magic love, how charming
   To catch hearts by surprise!
To wake them like the dawn,
When spring-time is new-born.

In the bosquet of Pouzange
   I meet my faithful loves.

>   They murmur in the leafage,
>   Sweet tender-throated doves.
>   They sing the whole day long,
>   And love is all their song.

But there is a sadder note which makes itself heard in these songs of love in Poitou, as elsewhere,— the lamentation of the maiden who has listened too fondly to the words of her shepherd lover, and experienced his faithlessness. She must hide at home with her shame, and sadly find that only her dog is faithful.

IT WAS THE SPRING SIX MONTHS AGO.

> It was the spring six months ago,
> And in the fresh, green fields below,
>   My bleating flock around me fed,
>   While watching them I spun my thread,
> And naught of sin or shame did know.
>
> But Colin came one evening fair,
> With tender words beguiled me there;
>   "Dear shepherdess, come take my arm,
>   Lest lonely roads should bring you harm,
> And ghosts or wolves in darkness scare."
>
> In his my trusting hand I place,
> While love invades me with its grace;
>   I could not check his passion's strength,
>   And wished the road of greater length,
> While listening with a blushing face.

But Colin has a faithless mind,
Inconstant as the changing wind.
   While I shamefaced must hide at home,
   Vainly asking when my love will come,
But my dog alone is true and kind.

The conscription, which compels the peasant, who has drawn the fatal number, to leave his native fields and his mistress, is an important and disturbing influence in the rural life of France, and finds a frequent place in its folk-song. Sometimes it is taken gayly, and the lover departs in high spirits, singing along the road to the garrison with his companions, and promising fidelity to his mistress to whom he hopes soon to return. It is thus in the gay song Voici l'Hiver Passé.

THE WINTER IT IS PAST.

The winter it is past,
   The freezing frost and snow,
The springtime it has come,
   And to the fields we go.

Above, upon the hilltop,
   The flowers bright and blue,
The little singing birds
   Their joyful songs renew.

They say in tender tones,
   In language sweet and clear,

> That every pretty maiden
>   Should have a lover dear.
>
> But mine has gone away,
>   A soldier's trade to learn
> In service at Bordeaux,
>   But he will soon return.
>
> We go, my comrades brave,
>   Let's bid our girls good-by,
> Give them a parting kiss,
>   And tell them not to cry.
>
> With knapsack on the back,
>   We make a brave convoy.
> We march along the road
>   With gallant songs of joy.
>
> At Bordeaux, when you come,
>   And other girls you see,
> You'll make another choice,
>   And think no more of me.
>
> When I am at Bordeaux,
>   Fond letters I will write,
> And give them to the clouds,
>   That pass with bosoms white.
>
> There will be within them,
>   In letters deep and clear,
> That I will always be
>   Your lover true and dear.

But the circumstances are not always so cheerful nor the songs so gay. There is a tragedy, when, moved by an irresistible longing, the unfortunate conscript has deserted the ranks, been captured by his comrades, and condemned to suffer the penalty of his weakness in a shameful death. The old songs have many subjects of that kind, whose memory lingers, although the penalty for desertion is now less severe. One of them is Le Deserteur, whose deeply plaintive air, and the melopœism of its verse, as well as its simple tragedy, have kept it alive.

THE DESERTER.

"For eight long years within the troop I served,
 Without a furlough to relieve my pain.
The longing took me to desert the ranks,
 To my fair land to turn my steps again.

"I had a luckless meeting on my way,
 Three grenadiers before me made a halt.
With handcuffs hard and cold they bound my hands,
 And led me to Bordeaux to a prison vault.

"Ah, is it then for love of a brown maid,
 That in a cell I lie in dismal mood;
My only couch the hard planks of the floor,
 Water and black bread my only drink and food."

But when the maiden heard these words of grief,
 Both night and day she walked her love to see.
"Courage, my dear love," through the grate she said,
 "I will find out a way to rescue thee.

"I will run out, and seek your captain kind,
　Your captain kind, and your brave colonel too.
I will beseech them, and implore a pardon,
　I will give them gold to free my lover true!"

"I am deeply grieved, my little shepherdess,
　That for this grenadier you should moan and cry.
Before the court of war he must soon appear,
　And at the drum will be condemned to die!"

When the maiden heard the cruel words he said,
　Her cheeks grew white that were so rosy red.
The captain threw his arm around her waist,
　And kindly bade her lift her drooping head.

"Fair shepherdess, take me for your lover,
　I will love you well, and free your heart from pain."
Tears within her eyes, and kerchief to her face,
　"No, no," she said, "I cannot love again."

But the soldier or the sailor after long years of service gets leave to return to his home on a furlough or a discharge. Sometimes he is welcomed by his aged parents or his faithful wife, who recognize him with joyful surprise, in spite of his rags and wounds; and sometimes he finds that his long absence has wrought fatal changes, that his parents are dead, or his wife, deceived by false news of his death, has married again. Incidents of this latter kind are familiar in folk-song, but there is none where the story is more simply and dramatically told, or where the conduct of the unfortunate husband shows such pathetic refinement of feeling, than in La Femme du Marin, which is one of the best-known and popular of the old songs of Poitou. The air is charmingly soft and melancholy, and the words display a skill in melody which the most accomplished poet might envy. A more felicitous verse can hardly be found in the whole annals of folk-song than this:—

> Quand le marin revient de guerre,
>   Tout doux.
> Quand le marin revient de guerre,
>   Tout doux.
> Tout mal chaussé, tout mal vetu,
> Pauvre marin du reviens tu ?
>   Tout doux.

It is hardly necessary to apologize for the imperfection of an attempt to render such a flower of poetry into another language.

THE WIFE OF THE MARINE.[1]

> When the marine came from the war,
>   Good and kind.
> When the marine came from the war,
>   Good and kind.
> With ragged coat and battered shoe.

---

[1] I have translated marin as "marine" instead of sailor, as in the last verse it is said that he goes back to his "regiment."

Poor marine, from whence come you?
    Good and kind.

Madame, I come from the war,
    Good and kind.
Madame, I come from the war,
    Good and kind.
Bring me now a brimming glass,
That I may drink it as I pass,
    Good and kind.

The brave marine begins to drink,
    Good and kind.
The brave marine begins to drink,
    Good and kind.
Drinks and sings a ballad gay,
While madame wipes the tears away,
    Good and kind.

What troubles you, my fair hostess?
    Good and kind.
What troubles you, my fair hostess?
    Good and kind.
Do you regret the kindly glass,
That you give me as I pass?
    Good and kind.

I don't regret my good white wine,
    Good and kind.
I don't regret my good white wine,
    Good and kind.
A husband's loss bedims my eyes,
For in your looks his image lies,
    Good and kind.

Ah, tell me now, my fair hostess,
    Good and kind.
Ah, tell me now, my fair hostess,
    Good and kind.
Children three he left behind,
But now three more with you I find,
    Good and kind.

I had a letter from the war,
    Good and kind.
I had a letter from the war,
    Good and kind.
Which said my brave marine was dead,
I thought it true; again I wed,
    Good and kind.

The brave marine drank out his glass,
    Good and kind.
The brave marine drank out his glass,
    Good and kind.
Without a word, while soft tears flowed,
To his corps went back his road,
    Good and kind.

SOME ANCIENT PORTUGUESE BALLADS.

The larger and more important literature of Spain has naturally drawn a wider attention than that of its smaller neighbor in the Iberian peninsula. The great achievements of Spanish genius in the era of its intellectual efflorescence have compelled the intellectual world to study its language and familiarize itself with its literature. And not only have the great works of Cervantes and Calderon and Lope de Vega been studied and criticised, and reproduced in all the cultivated languages of Europe, but the treasures of popular Spanish poetry, with their rich elements of chivalry and romantic passion, have been carefully studied and exemplified by foreign scholars, and been the inspiration of foreign poets and translators. Hardly any country in Europe has a more valuable collection of popular poetry in the times of its military and intellectual greatness, or which more thoroughly illustrates its history or the characteristics of its national temperament. The long chronicles of the Cid, and the ballad narratives of the exploits of the heroes of the great struggles for the expulsion of the Moors, form in themselves a rich body of national poetry, but they are supplemented by an immense number of episodical ballads relating to events in national history, and lyrical poems and songs expressing the strong feeling and intellectual energy of the people. Many scholars and poets of eminence in European countries have devoted themselves to the reproduction of these Spanish national poems in their own languages, and in England during the early part of the present century there was a strong bent of scholarship in that direction, induced to a considerable extent, probably, by the national interest in the Peninsular war. Southey, Scott, and John Hookham Frere gave admirable translations of Spanish national poems, and the spirited versions of ancient Spanish ballads by Lockhart have been justly considered a permanent addition to English poetry.

But no such degree of attention has been paid to Portuguese literature, although it possesses the same national characteristics as the Spanish, and is not inferior, except in volume, as regards the product of popular poetry and folk-song. This was natural enough. Except the great poem of Camoens, Portuguese literature possesses no masterpiece to compel the attention of the civilized world, and the product of its national genius is not of the bulk and importance of that of Spain. Its national characteristics were similar, so that independent study was not incited by original features, while the difference in language was sufficient to be a barrier to all except special scholars. The country was in a measure overwhelmed and overshadowed by Spain, although possessing independent and interesting features of its own, and has been regarded as a province rather than as an original country. Very little attention has been paid in foreign countries to Portuguese popular literature, although some French and German scholars have included it in their studies, and there is no volume in English, so far as I am aware, which deals with it. At the same time it is well worth attention in its richness and value in all the qualities which make a high order of popular poetry, and in those elements of chivalric feeling, dramatic incident, and intensity of passion which characterize Spanish poetry of the same period. Fortunately Portugal itself has shared in that interest, which has spread through all the civilized countries of Europe in ancient popular literature and folk-song, and its national scholars have devoted a painstaking care and interest to collecting and elucidating its ancient ballads. The pioneer in this work was Almeida Garrett, himself a distinguished poet, who, being compelled to take refuge in England by the political disturbances of 1820, came under the influence of Sir Walter Scott as regards the work which he had done for the national literature of Scotland. Like Scott he at first wrote imitations of the old ballads with their literary style and phrases. These, like all other imitations of ancient ballads, although full of strength and poetical power, had not the genuine naturalness of antiquity and the inimitable flavor of primitive art. Later, on his return to Portugal, Almeida Garrett set himself to work to collect the ancient Portuguese ballads, as Scott had done those of the Scottish border, and was almost equally successful. The backwardness of the Portuguese peasantry in education, and their comparative seclusion from the influences of modern civilization in their mountains and valleys, contributed very much to the preservation of their ancient ballads, and even to-day they are a part of the oral literature of the country. There were of course many ancient ballads, in written and printed forms, which were preserved in libraries and in the papers of old families, but the great bulk of Almeida Garrett's collection was derived from oral tradition. He followed the example of Scott in uniting the best forms of varying versions into a complete and harmonious whole, and it is hardly doubtful that he also supplied an occasional wanting or imperfect line. But his general faithfulness and respect for the originals have been abundantly proved by the work of later collectors. The popular poetry of Portugal owes no less to Almeida Garrett than that of Scotland does to Scott, and he inculcated a pride in national history and national literature by his genius, as well as rescued the remains of ancient popular poetry by his painstaking care. Since his time he has been followed by other Portuguese scholars, who have worked under the restrictions of more absolute faithfulness and historic research imposed by the modern study of folk-lore. Notably Signor Braga has published two very valuable volumes, Romanceiro Geral, relating to the popular poetry of Portugal, and the Cantos Populares do Archipelago Açoriario, the songs of the Azore islands, whose seclusion from the world has been very favorable to the preservation of the ancient popular poetry and folk-lore. There are others who have made national collections, and the folk-songs of the various provinces, so that now the popular poetry of Portugal has been as carefully gathered and preserved as that of any other nation of Europe.

The popular poetry of Portugal had its period of efflorescence contemporaneous with that of Spain, and covered the period of its national energy and enterprise. The oldest specimens now extant are not considered to date beyond the fifteenth century, although, of course, they may have derived their origin from still more ancient ballads. The greater part is included within the two centuries following, when the national mind still preserved the spring and energy which had accomplished such great achievements in navigation and enterprise, and before its spirit had been crushed into the narrow bounds of a restricted and decaying province. Contrary, however, to the condition of the national poetry in Spain, the allusions to the actual events of recorded history are somewhat rare, and, although the actions of kings and national heroes make some figure, for the most part they relate to popular traditions, which have but a vague connection with national history. In style and manner, however, they bear a close resemblance to the Spanish popular poems, and in many instances they appear but as slightly differing variants, although it is doubtful which may have been the original, the Spanish or the Portuguese. The ballad of Dom Yanno, which is a specimen of the longer popular romances, is similar, except in its termination, to the Castilian romance known under the title of the Count Alarcos, and which has been translated by Lockhart under the title of Count Alarcos and the Infanta Solisa. In the Spanish romance the count actually fulfills the commands of the king by murdering his spouse, but before her death she cites the king and the infanta to appear within thirty days before the judgment seat of God, and it is accomplished by their deaths in that time. There are numerous variants to the ballad in Spanish popular literature, and it has been made the subject of dramas by Lope de Vega and others. Its connection with actual history is unknown.

DOM YANNO.

The princess wept and wept again; the reason for her tears
And that her life had little joy within her royal house,
Was that her father had forgot for slowly passing years
To dower her in marriage with some rich and noble spouse.

Her mourning was so deep one night, the king woke in his bed.
"What troubles you, my daughter dear, why do you weep and mourn?"
"Of your three daughters, royal sire, alone I am not wed.
Therefore my days are dark and dull; therefore I am forlorn."

"What remedy is there for that? I'm not the one to blame;
Ambassadors from Aquitaine and lords from Normandy,
When with noble marriage proffers in suppliance they came,
You would not hearken to at all, nor treat with courtesy."

"Of all the nobles of my court not one is there I see,
Except Count Yanno, who in wealth and lineage of pride

Can for a single instant seem a worthy spouse for thee,
And he has taken to his house a fair and noble bride."

"O noble father of my soul, you've named the very one.
If he already has a wife, and even children too,
He owes another pledge to me, for my weak heart he won.
He gave to me his solemn word, and I believed it true."

The king sent summons to the count to come where he awaits.
He had not thought what he should do, or e'en what he
  should say.
"'T is but a single moment since I left the palace gates,
And now the king demands me back; what does it mean, I
  pray?"

Count Yanno enters in the hall; the king straight to him goes.
"My lord, I humbly kiss your hands; what is your royal
  will?"
"You may kiss them for the honor the king on thee bestows,
In wedlock take my daughter's hand, and your sworn troth
  fulfill."

Count Yanno, when he heard these words, was struck with
  mortal dread.
"My royal master, I've a wife with whom I live in bliss."
"Go kill your wife without delay, and then my daughter wed."
"What! kill my wife, so innocent! What black command is
  this!"

"Be silent, Count, your insolence I will not suffer now.
One cannot trick a royal maid like any simple slave."
"My lord, before your righteous rage in penitence I bow,
That I may pay the debt alone is all I humbly crave."

"That I should kill an innocent, who's never done a wrong,
Such deadly treason would o'erwhelm my soul with shame and sin.
The life of earth in punishment to justice would belong,
And in the life beyond the grave no pardon could I win."

"The Countess is a burden here, and therefore must she die;
In that gilt basin bring her head, all dripping with its gore."
Count Yanno left the cruel king, his soul in agony,
And followed the dark page, whose arms the fatal basin bore.

The page was clad in mourning garb, the Count in sad array,
As if in pain of parting breath his heart with anguish swelled,
The Countess ran to meet him, as she saw him far away;
Her husband and her little child in one embrace she held.

"Well come — well come, Count, for my joy;" but not a word he said,
He mounted slowly up the steps, and locked and barred the door;
Then bade the wondering servants the supper table spread:
The household marveled at a mien they'd never seen before,

They did not touch the food or wine, but sat in sad unrest.
The tears welled from Count Yanno's eyes; he bent to kiss the child,
That to his mother's warm, soft breast his rosy lips had prest:
The infant turned to meet the kiss, and like an angel smiled.

To see that mingled smile and kiss, her heart in sobs broke out,
The echoes of her bursting grief filled all the lofty room:

"What troubles you, my best beloved; resolve this dreadful
   doubt,
What is the order of the king that fills you so with gloom?"

The Count choked down his sudden sobs, he could no answer
   make.
She clasped his neck and on his mouth she pressed a frantic
   kiss.
"Take from my heart this agony I suffer for your sake,
Let me partake your sorrow, dear, and you shall share my
   bliss."

The woeful pair from table rose, and sought in bed to rest,
But slumber came not to their eyes, to give their pains
   relief.
"By the good God in heaven above, and Virgin Mary blest,
My very life I'd sooner give than see you in such grief."

"May death revenge such black command; perish his tyr-
   anny!
My Count, I do not understand what 'tis he bids thee do;
Upon my life and soul, my love, reveal it now to me,
This dreadful shadow of ill fate that comes between us
   two."

"The fate of an ill-fated one, and no help can there be,
The king commands that I kill thee, and the Infanta wed."
Scarce had these dreadful words been spoke in stifled agony
When the unhappy Countess fell, as if her life had fled.

God did not give her death's relief, tho' better she had
   died
For anguish deeper far than death recalled life to her heart,

"Wait, wait, Count Yanno, kill me not, but let me go and hide
In my dear father's distant house, where I can dwell apart.

"There I will live a maid again, and keep my true troth-
plight ;
There I will rear this infant, and guard him from all sin ;
Though sorrow lies between us two, he 'll be my dear delight,
And I 'll be faithful to my love as I have always been."

"How can that be, my best beloved, it is the king's black will
Within that gilded basin there to see your severed head."
"Wait, wait, Count Yanno, kill me not, I have a refuge still ;
The cloistered nuns will guard me, when to their cells I 've
fled.

"My bread be measured by the ounce, my drink quench not
my thirst,
Then speedily my death will come, nor will the princess
know."
"How can that be, my best beloved, since in that basin curst
I must thy severed head before the king and princess show."

"Enclose me in a dungeon dark, where neither sun nor moon
Shall light the hours I count by sighs until my life has fled."
"How can that be, my best beloved ? the hour will come full
soon
When in that gilded basin there the king must see your
head."

The king knocked harshly at the door as these last words
were said :
"If the Countess still is living, quick, quick, make haste to
slay."

"The Countess says her orisons, but soon she will be dead,
And in a single moment's space her soul will pass away."

"Oh, let me say a final prayer to bid the world good-night."
"Make haste to say it, my beloved, for daybreak I can see."
"Oh, God and Virgin Mary blest, I cannot pray aright;
It is not death afflicts me so, but shameful treachery.

"I pity you more than myself, for your base cowardice ;
With your own hand you take my life, though reason there
    is none
Except the wicked princess' hand will pay the shameful price.
May God forgive you at the hour you stand before his
    throne !

"Oh, let me say my last farewell to all I've loved so dear,
The flower of Alexandria, the roses red and white,
The little tender violets, the fountain waters clear,
I've tended you with love and care ; the princess' hand will
    blight.

"Give me my child, fruit of my womb, in my weak arms to
    hold,
That he may feed upon the breast that swells with its last
    breath.
It is my blood that he will drink, that runs so faint and cold.
Drink, little infant, drink the milk that's tinged with bitter
    death.
To-day you have a mother dear, who loves you tenderly,
To-morrow a step-mother harsh, of loftiest degree."

The great church bell tolls heavily. Ah, Jesus, who is dead ?
The infant's lips by miracle this wondrous answer made :

"The princess, choked with wickedness; her soul in sin has fled;
To part such dear and faithful loves God's holy might forbade!"

The ballad of The Ship Catharine is one of the best known and most popular among the folk-songs of Portugal. Various attempts have been made by Almeida Garrett, Braga, and others to attach it to some historical event, but without satisfactory success, and, indeed, its character is such that it is apparent that it belongs rather to the order of indefinite romance. The incidents in regard to the drawing of the lots to see who shall be eaten, and the ascent of the sailor to look for land, are to be found in the folk-songs of various maritime nations. One of them has been found in Brittany and has been preserved by M. Luzel in the Gwerzion Breiz-Izel. It relates that a vessel, which had been voyaging for twenty-seven years upon the high seas, naturally fell short of provisions, and the crew were compelled to think of eating each other:

"And when they had drawn for the short straw, it was the master of the vessel to whom it fell — Great God, is it possible that my sailors will eat me?"

"Little page, little page, you who are quick and nimble — go to the top of the main mast to find out where we are."

"And he mounted singing, and descended weeping — I have been to the top of the main mast and have not seen any land."

"Go again to the top of the main mast to find out where we are — It will be for the last time."

"He mounted weeping, and he descended singing — I believe that we are restored to land — I have seen the tower of Babylon," etc.

A ballad, The Little Midshipman, in the popular songs of Provence, is very similar in incident and language to The Ship Catharine, with a change in the localities, the midshipman seeing Toulon and Marseilles instead of the coasts of Portugal and Spain. In later French folk-song the ballad has become a burlesque after the fashion of Malbrook, and is known as Il etait un Petit Navire. This in its turn was developed in the after-dinner song of Thackeray, "There were three sailors of Bristol city," and is an instance of the persistence of folk-song, even though changed in form and purpose. The supernatural element in The Ship Catharine is rare in Portuguese popular poetry.

THE SHIP CATHARINE.

The Catharine was a gallant ship,
On which a wonder did befall

I 'll tell the story as it happ'd,
  If you will listen one and all.

The ship had ploughed the long, salt seas,
  Until a year and day had gone.
Their stores of food were eaten out,
  And beef and biscuit they had none.

They tried to soak a shoe to eat,
  Its skin so hard they could not gnaw.
For who should serve his mates for food,
  In turns the deadly lot they draw.

The shortest straw the captain drew.
  I wot it caused him bitter pain :
"Little sailor, climb the top-mast,
  And look for Portugal or Spain."

"The coast of Portugal or Spain
  On either side I cannot see ;
But seven swords drawn from their sheaths
  Shine bright and bare to slaughter thee."

"Higher, higher, my little sailor,
  On the top-gallant take your stand,
Try and see the coast of Portugal,
  Or of Spain the shining strand."

"What reward, my gallant captain !
  Both Spain and Portugal I see,
I also see three lovely maidens
  Seated beneath an orange tree.

"The eldest of them sews a seam,
  Another spins a shining thread,

The fairest sits between the two,
    And hangs in tears her lovely head."

"My darling daughters are all the three,
    I love them dearer than my life.
For your reward, my little sailor,
    The loveliest shall be your wife."

"I do not wish your darling daughter;
    The cost of love would be my bane."
"I 'll give you gold beyond your count."
    "It cost you too much strife to gain."

"I 'll give to you my courier white,
    A nobler never felt the rein."
"I do not want your courier white,
    It cost you too much toil to train."

"I 'll give to you my gallant ship,
    Upon the seas to sail at will."
"I do not want your gallant ship,
    To navigate I have no skill."

"What reward then, little sailor,
    Do you demand that I should pay?"
"I want your soul, my gallant captain,
    Your soul with me to take away."

"Demon, your claim I do deny.
    I will not yield my soul to thee.
My soul belongs to God above,
    My body I 'll give to the sea."

An angel caught him in her arms,
    And drew him from the boiling spray.

> The demon flew ; at eve the ship
>   Was anchored safe within the bay.

It is somewhat singular that with all the enterprise of the Portuguese upon the sea during their period of national glory, their perilous and adventurous navigations, and their many successful engagements in marine warfare, there should be so few ballads relating to the sea-faring exploits. There is one, however, Don Juan d'Armada, which seems to relate to some definite victory over the Turks, but the occasion and even the name of the hero are not recorded in authentic history. It has many features, however, which would indicate that it was the account of an actual event.

DON JUAN D'ARMADA.

His Majesty, God guard him, gave order for the fleet
To sail at early daybreak the Turkish foe to meet.
The admiral's ship at midnight fires the signal gun,
And to the quay distracted the maids and matrons run.
Sons and lovers they embrace ; they weep with bitter tears ;
Their voices break with sorrow; their hearts are swelled with
    fears.

On board the busy vessels the noises grow more loud,
The masters and the boatswains rush eager in the crowd,
The captain of each frigate his silver whistle blows,
And on the lofty yard-arms the sailors stand in rows.
The white sails drop and belly out before the swelling breeze ;

The white foam curls along the prow ; the brave fleet seeks
    the seas.

Don Juan held his course before the favoring gale,
At midday to the watchman he gave a roaring hail.
"Get higher to the mast-head !" he shouted strong and loud.
The sailor quickly mounted the thin and shaking shroud.
"Sail ho, sail ho," he shouted, "a mighty fleet 's ahead,
Across the whole horizon the line of ships is spread."

A Spanish renegade commanded that proud fleet
Who by his beard had sworn Don Juan to defeat.
Don Juan trusted Christ and made a solemn vow,
The cross within his arms, and standing on the prow.
Oh, Son of Virgin Mary, give us the heart to fight
Those dogs of heathen pride, and scatter them in flight.

The midday sun was bright, when the two fleets grappled
    close,
And from the roaring cannon a blinding smoke arose,
The bullets crashed in splinters and shattered plank and
    beam.
To the sea the scuppers poured a hot and crimson stream.
The bleeding corpses lay in heaps upon the reeking decks,
With tattered sails and rudderless the ships were drifting
    wrecks.

The Turkish captain's galley swung helpless on the sea.
Of its three hundred sailors were left but forty-three,
Along its shattered gunwales the masts and hamper drag,
And weltering in the wake trails its dishonored flag.
The Turkish fleet was beaten, and fled with sail and oar,
Until it reached the harbor and anchored by the shore.

Said the Sultan, "How came this? Who struck this deadly
    blow?"
"'T was Don Juan d'Armada, who brought our pennons low."
"I do not mourn the galleys, for I can build me more,
But I regret my sailors that never will see shore.
For Don Juan d'Armada give him the honor due;
He is the king of captains, since he has conquered you."

As in the Spanish romances, there are numerous allusions in the Portuguese ballads to the constant warfare waged with the Barbary corsairs, and the adventures of the unhappy captives who fell into their hands and were reduced to cruel servitude. A favorite theme with the ballad-writers was the rescue of the captive through the means of the Moorish damsel, who had fallen in love with him as she saw him laboring at his tasks. No doubt some such adventures actually happened, and at any rate the theme was one which appealed strongly to the imagination of the popular poets. This one ends with a touch of sentiment which might seem a modern addition, if the authenticity of the whole ballad was not vouched for by so careful a collector as Braga.

THE CAPTIVE.

I sailed from Hamburg port one morn
    Upon a bonny caravel.
'T was neither war nor peace at sea,
    When pirate Moors upon us fell.

They took me as a slave to sell,
    Unto their country of Salee,
But neither Moor nor Mussulman
    Would give a silver groat for me.

'T was only a false Jewish dog,
    Who wished to have me for his slave,
He made my life a bitter pain,
    And beat me like a scurvy knave.

All day I wove esparto grass,
    At night I turned the hard corn mill,
A wooden gag between my jaws
    Lest of the meal I 'd steal my fill.

But fortune brought me a kind dame,
    Who pitied the sad life I led,
She sent me from her table rich
    Fresh meat and wine and good white bread.

She gave me all things that I asked,
    And something I asked not, as well,
Within Jewessa's arms I wept,
    But not for her the salt tears fell.

"Christian, you need not weep," she said,
    "I know your grief ere it is told."
"But how can I my home regain
    Without a single piece of gold?"

"If 't is to buy a horse you need,
    I 'll give to you my pretty mare,
You need not wait to find a ship,
    But take the shallop anchored there."

"Fair dame, 't is not a horse will serve,
  For far is Ceuta and Castille,
To take a ship and run away,
  Would be your father's slave to steal."

"Oh, take this purse of yellow silk,
  My mother dying gave to me,
The golden pieces it contains
  Will richly pay your ransom fee.

"And when at home returned again,
  To Christian maidens you can say
How Jewish hearts can sacrifice
  And show a deeper love than they."

As thus she spoke, the master came.
  "Oh, master," said I, "God be praised,
Good news has come across the sea,
  My friends the ransom price have raised."

"Ah, Christian, what is that you say,
  Many cruzadoes it will need.
Who gives you enough of gold
  To pay the heavy ransom's meed?"

"My sisters twain have sent me part,
  The other I had kept in store.
An angel has brought me the gold,
  An angel bright from heaven's door."

"Hearken, Christian, change your faith,
  And you shall wed my daughter dear,
My goods and wealth shall all be thine,
  And joy and peace surround you here."

"I will not be a cursed Jew,
　　Nor heathen Turk of grace denied,
Nor will I change for all your wealth
　　The faith of Jesus crucified."

"Why are you pale, Rachael, my girl,
　　Beloved child, tell me the truth;
Have you been brought to shameful harm
　　By this accursed Christian youth?"

"Oh, let the Christian youth go free,
　　For his amend I have no claim,
If my flower of love he's had,
　　I gave it, and he's not to blame."

He shut her in a dungeon tower,
　　Which he with heavy stone blocks made,
That the base Moors might never know
　　That shame had touched a Jewish maid.

Oh, mandolin, my mandolin,
　　Rest silent hung upon the wall,
My longing love across the sea
　　Is borne away beyond recall.

The Faithful Paladin has a more tragical ending for the captive. The ballad had its origin in the province of Algarve, but there are several variants in Portuguese as well as similar ballads in Spanish. Calderon has made the theme the subject of a drama under the title of The Constant Prince, relating to the captivity and sufferings of Don Fernando, heir to the throne of Portugal, who was captured by the Moors in 1438.

THE FAITHFUL PALADIN.

Adventured in a Moorish land,
    A paladin, heartstrong and brave,
Fell into Miramolin's hands,
    To serve him as a captive slave.

The Moorish king a daughter had,
    More white and fair than jasmine flower.
Her eyes with sparkling light were glad,
    And youth and bloom her beauty's dower.

To Safim as she looked one day
    Celima saw the captive knight,
With pensive gaze turned far away,
    And sadness in his empty sight.

The touch she felt within her heart
    She sought with shamefaced care to hide,
None guessed the wound that gave the smart,
    Or heard her weeping when she cried.

Since then her pastimes had no zest,
    Nor could she even peace regain,
The longing love that filled her breast
    Grew every day a deeper pain.

Upon the terrace hours and hours
    She sat and watched the slave below
Dig at his task among the flowers,
    In summer sunshine's burning glow.

At last her longing broke her pride,
  She told her passion on her knees.
He silent stood, and only sighed
  For her he loved beyond the seas.

Faithful and true to his fond love,
  It fenced his heart with triple shield,
Not all Celima's charms could move
  A more than pitying grace to yield.

"My gold and jewels shall be thine,
  If only you but wish it so,
And with your freedom give me mine;
  Tell me, Christian, yes or no."

"I wish no jewels from your hand,
  Or aught that may belong to thee,
Some one will come from my far land,
  And for my ransom pay the fee."

"Then let me be your humble slave
  To serve you wheresoe'er you go.
No better fortune can I crave,
  Tell me, Christian, yes or no."

"My humble slave you must not be,
  A better fortune is your due;
How came your love to fix on me,
  Who have no heart to give to you?"

"My God and father I'll forswear,
  And only yours will seek to know;
Every curse of heaven I'll dare,
  Tell me, Christian, yes or no."

"Your love and riches tempt me not.
    Both love and riches wait for me.
Accursed be the fatal lot
    That brought me o'er the sad, salt sea.

"I spurn a soul that turns to God,
    A heart for me that suffers pain.
Be happy in the paths you've trod,
    And love a youth who loves again."

When these sad words the captive said,
    With sudden wrath she turned away.
In seven days the knight was dead.
    Was it her deed? No one can say.

The epoch of the Crusades is beyond the limit of the popular ballads which have been preserved, although it is probable that they may have had their foundation in originals of that date. The story of the return of the spouse from the Holy Land, and his making himself known after various trials of his wife's fidelity, is a common one in the ballads of all European nations, and is of a character to appeal to the dramatic instincts of the popular poets. Close resemblances to the ballad of The Fair Princess can be found in German, French, and Spanish popular poetry, and the theme itself of course dates back to the return of Ulysses, and to the ballads which were the origin of the Odyssey.

THE FAIR PRINCESS.

The princess sat in her garden fair;
With a golden comb she combed her hair.
She raised her eyes to the azure bay.
A brave fleet bore in with pennons gay.

"Good captain, say, in the Holy Land
　Have you seen my spouse with his brave band?"
"In Holy Land is many a knight.
　With what point device was he bedight?"

"His steed bore saddle of silver gilt
　The cross of Christ was his gold sword hilt."
"A knight with these I saw bravely fall
　In fierce assault on a city's wall."

"A wretched widow I have become
　To mourn and weep in a ruined home,
I have three daughters, lovely and sage,
But spouseless and weak in orphanage."

"What gift to him who returns your spouse?"
"All the gold and silver in the house."
"Of gold and silver I have no need,
　Some other guerdon must be my meed."

"I have three great mills; all shall be thine.
　They grind white wheat and benzoin fine,
　The delicate flour, so finely wrought,
　The royal stewards have always sought."

"For your three mills I have no desire,
　Some other reward must pay my hire."

"My roof tile of gold and ivory."
"Your gold and iv'ry tiles are not for me."

"My daughters fair, you shall have them all;
Two to serve you in your banquet hall;
The third and fairest shall be your bride,
In love's nest to slumber by your side."

"Princess, your fair daughters count for nought,
A costlier gift is in my thought."
"I have nothing more to offer thee;
No other gift can you ask of me."

"But I only ask, and you can spare
The simple gift of your body fair."
"A fouler insult knight ne'er gave.
Haste, vassals, and scourge this loathly knave."

"The wedding ring with diamonds bright,
We broke in twain on our bridal night.
Where is the half you have kept so dear?
The other half you can see it here."

"How many tears you have made me shed!
How slow the lingering years have fled!
What pains and griefs lie in your debt!
When bliss like this cannot forget."

The ballad of Dom Duardos and Flerida has an antique flavor in its simplicity and indefiniteness, as in its element of imaginative poetry, which would lead to a belief in its ancient origin, dating beyond the acquirement of more accomplished art in the popular poets. A similar ballad is to be found in the Castilian.

DOM DUARDOS AND FLERIDA.

'T was in the month of April,
  The day before May day,
When roses red, and lilies white,
  Are blooming bright and gay.

The night was calm and cloudless,
  With golden stars arrayed,
The Infanta, fair Flerida,
  In her wide garden strayed.

"God guard you, tender flowers,
  Great joy you've given me;
I go to a strange land;
  Such is my fate's decree.

"If my father seeks me,
  He who loves me well;
Tell him that love has drawn me
  Within its fatal spell.

"Tell him that fateful love
  Has seized me in its hold;
I know not where I go,
  And none to me has told."

Then Dom Duardos spoke:
  "Oh, weep not so, my dear,
In the great realm of England
  Are fairer things than here.

"There are more limpid streams,
　　And gardens yet more fair.
　A thousand flowers blooming,
　　And scenting all the air.

"Three hundred maids shall serve,
　　And all of noble strain,
　And palaces of silver,
　　Where you shall nobly reign.

"With emeralds of green,
　　And finest Turkish gold,
　Upon the shining walls
　　The story shall be told

"How, to do you honor,
　　I fought Primaleon.
　I did not fear his strength,
　　When your bright glances shone."

When fair Flerida heard,
　　She wiped her tears away.
　And hand in hand they went
　　To where his galleys lay.

The fifty galleys brave
　　Moved out upon the deep,
　And to their chiming oars
　　Flerida fell asleep,
　In Dom Duardos' arms,
　　Whose heart with joy did leap.

Know all men that are born,
　　How sure is fate's decree,

> From neither love nor death
> Can mortal man be free.

Ballads on the subject of the slaying a would-be ravisher with his own arms are common in popular poetry, and striking examples are found in Scotch, French, and Spanish. There are several variants in Portuguese of The Pilgrim Maid, but the best is that furnished by Almeida Garrett.

THE PILGRIM MAID.

Adown the lofty mountain green
    The pilgrim maid descends :
No fairer and no purer maid
    To sacred station wends.

Her long robe catches in the thorns,
    That strew the grassy mat,
Her lovely eyes are downward cast,
    And hidden by her hat.

A knight pursues her footsteps fast,
    With evil in his eyes,
But he can hardly reach her side,
    Though his best speed he tries.

At last he's caught her, as she stops
    Beside the olive tree,
That at the holy hermit's door
    Stands fair and tall to see.

She leans against the sacred wood, —
  "By God and Saint Marie,
This holy place should be my guard,
  Oh, do no wrong to me."

The false knight was too base of heart
  To feel God's sacred grace.
He throws his arms around her form
  In strong and fierce embrace.

In mad and furious wrestle,
  Their struggling arms are wound;
The maiden's strength is crushed by his:
  She 's cast upon the ground.

But as she falls she pulls the dirk,
  That in his belt she spies;
She strikes it deep to his false heart,
  And out the black blood flies.

"Oh, pilgrim maid, I beg and pray
  By God and Saint Marie,
Tell not of my dishonored death,
  Or how you 've punished me."

"I 'll tell the tale in your own land,
  And in mine vaunt it too,
How such a villain, false and base,
  With his own blade I slew."

She pulls the cord that swings the bell;
  It makes a solemn din.
"Oh, hermit, pray that God may save
  This soul that dies in sin,

> And grant a grave in holy ground
> His body to lie in."

The Portuguese ballads, which relate to domestic tragedies, without reference to historic events, are numerous, and very frequently of a high order of merit. They have the characteristics of folk-poetry in their dramatic interjections and irregularities, but often have a consistency and strength not found in the more romantic ballads. The Death-Bed Marriage is a specimen of this class.

THE DEATH-BED MARRIAGE.

From the frontier of Castille the bitter news has flown,
The brave Dom Juan is dying; how his dear love will moan;
Three doctors grave were summoned, the most renowned for skill,
If they to life restore him gold will their purses fill.

The youngest two declared that the malady was slight;
But when the elder entered he saw with clearer light.
To the dying man he said, "You've but three hours to live,
To solemn thoughts and duties that short time you should give.

"One will serve to make your will, and purge your burdened soul,
One is for the sacrament, the church's sacred dole;
The third and last shall serve you, while tolls the passing bell
To see your best beloved, and say a last farewell."

While these sad words gave warning, fair Isabel stood by.
He turned to look upon her, with death mist in his eye.

"You have done well, my treasure, my death to look upon ;
I'll pray the Virgin Mary to heal the wrong I've done."

While thus he spoke in anguish, there came his mother dear,
"My darling son, what ails you, why is your soul in fear ?"
"Oh, mother, I am dying ; I have not long to last ;
Three hours to live they gave me, and one's already past."

"Son of my womb, consider, with death's hand on you laid,
Have you no debt of honor to pay some noble maid ?"
"Yes, mother, to my anguish I owe such debt of shame ;
That God may not in judgment condemn my soul to flame !"

"It is to Dona Isabel I owe that shameful debt ;
But a thousand cruzadoes a spouse for her will get."
"No gold nor silver money will pay for honor lost ;
Thy cruzadoes are worthless as leaves the wind has tost."

"I'll leave her to the doctors that they no skill may spare,
And you, my darling mother, will have her in your care,
A city for her dowry the day that she shall wed —
If any man refuse her, the axe shall have his head."

"The honor of a maid is not paid or bought with land,
Wed her, well-beloved, with your cold and dying hand,
That she may be your widow, and bear an honored name,
And though she weeps with sorrow it will not be for shame."

The ballad of Dom Aleixio, of which there are several versions, has a lightness of touch in the description of the masquerading maid, which is not often found in the popular ballads, although the conclusion is sufficiently tragic.

DOM ALEIXIO.

We are three sisters, young and gay,
    Our cheeks and eyes the likeness show;
In broidering we spend the day,
    Or teach each other how to sew.

The youngest, in her youth elate,
    The fancy took, one summer night,
To pass the orange garden gate,
    With two flambeaux to give her light.

She wore a pretty page's suit,
    That showed her shape so trim and neat;
In light, fair hands she held a lute,
    And colored shoes adorned her feet.

She strutted up and down the road,
    With mimic of a martial stride.
"Fair maidens here have their abode;
    Which of the three shall be my bride?"

Upon the balcony we leant,
    And laughed to see her gallant guise;
At length the torches' flame was spent;
    The moon had risen in the skies.

As to the gate her way she took
    When all her sportive tricks were done,
She saw with sudden startled look
    A hermit on a bench of stone.

"Father, what do you here?" she cries.
    He answered not, but stood upright;

So tall his stature seemed to rise,
  The stoutest heart would feel affright.

"If you're a demon, as you seem,
  This sacred cross bids you avaunt.
If your lost soul you would redeem,
  The holy priest shall masses chant."

"I'm not an imp from hell's domain;
  The holy cross I do not fear;
I'm not a soul that waits in pain,
  For a redeeming mass to hear.

"But Dom Aleixio's ghost am I
  To save you from a deadly strife;
There seven men in ambush lie,
  With naked swords to take your life."

"Indeed! then by the living God,
  And by the Virgin Mary's grace,
Were they twice seven, on the sod
  I would not yield a foot of space.

"Come on, come on, you sneaking band,
  And show your valiance in the light;
With good sword in each valiant hand,
  See, mine is ready for the fight.

"If weaponless is one of you,
  To him my own sword I will lend;
With this good dagger, keen and true,
  I can right well my life defend."

As thus she spoke these words of pride,
  The hermit off his robe did throw;

She snatched the dagger from his side,
    And pierced his heart with deadly blow.

"Oh, who has slain my lover true,
    That lies before me on the ground?"
"'T was you, my lady, only you
    Had fateful power to give the wound."

Rise up, Maria, from your knees,
    In vain in prayer your hands are crost,
The sobbing of the orange trees
    Bewails your soul, forever lost.

The ballad of Dom Pedro Menino was found by Signor Braga in the Azores islands, and is by him attributed to an actual historical event, the marriage of Dom Pedro Nino, a simple knight, to the infanta Beatrixe of Portugal; but, notwithstanding the similarity of names, it must be considered as at least doubtful.

DOM PEDRO MENINO.

The marquis had three gallant sons,
    Each one was handsome, brave and tall;
The king commanded them to come,
    And serve as pages in his hall.

The first put on the royal robe;
    The next the ribboned shoe-strings tied;
The third and youngest of the three
    His prentice hand as barber tried.

The princess saw his blooming face,
    And smiled on him with loving eye;
The King was told the shameful thing,
    And swore the daring page should die

He cast him in a dungeon cell,
    Within a tower great and strong.
While waiting there the fatal day,
    A huntsman chanced to pass along.

He saw Dom Pedro, as he passed.
    "Cousin, what do you there?" said he.
The prisoner answered through the grate,
    "I'm destined for the gallows tree.

"To-morrow morn I'm doomed to die,
    And to the ravens shall be fed,
All for a simple word of love
    That to the princess I had said."

The huntsman to the marquise goes,
    "I bring you news of woe and scorn,
Dom Pedro is condemned to die,
    As sure as comes to-morrow's morn."

The marquise mounted a fleet steed,
    And all her servants followed on,
Their mantles hung upon their arms,
    They had not time their cloaks to don.

"What do you in a prison cell?"
    "I'm doomed to the black gallows tree,
Because I kissed with love words light
    The royal maid, who smiled on me."

"Come, take your sweet-voiced mandolin,
    And sing in tune the while you play
The gentle song your father made
    In honor of St. John's fair day."

Is such a woman from God's hand?
    Her heart is harder than a stone.
Her son must die at morning's light;
    She bids him sing in joyous tone.

"O, what a lovely day,
    The bright day of St. John
When youths and maidens sweet
    Their shining garments don;
They smile as hand in hand,
    They move with dancing feet,
Some bearing blushing roses,
    And some the basil sweet.
How sad it is for me
    In prison cell to lie,
And never see the sun
    That sparkles in the sky."

The King, who rode his courser white,
    That he might view the royal chase,
Reined in his steed and loitered there
    With silent wonder in his face.

"What voice divine is that I hear,
    That fills the air with melody?
Is it the angels in the sky,
    Or magic sirens in the sea?"

"It is no angel in the sky,
    Nor magic siren in the sea,
It is Dom Pedro in the tower,
    Condemned to die for love of me.
I'd wish to have him for my spouse,
    If that the King would set him free."

"Bid the jailer hasten there;
    Take off his chains and let him go.
Take him, daughter, for your spouse,
    Since God himself has wished it so."

The ballad of Count Nillo may perhaps be attributed to the same real or imaginary origin as the preceding on account of some similarity in the name and the language, although the denouement is different. The trees which spring from the tombs of the unfortunate lovers and unite their branches is one of the most familiar images in folk-poetry, and hardly any collection of national ballads is without an example.

COUNT NILLO.

Count Nillo in the river halts to bathe his weary steed;
    While the thirsty stallion drinks the Count sings loud and high;
The evening shade had darkened down; the King's sight was not clear:
    The Infanta asked her heart if she would laugh or cry.

"Keep silent, daughter! hearken! What sweet song do you hear?
 Is it a heavenly angel, or siren of the sea?"
"It is no heavenly angel's song, or siren's magic voice,
 But Nillo, the Count Nillo, who comes to marry me."

"Who speaks of the Count Nillo, who dares to breathe his name?
 That traitor who defied me, and whom I have exiled."
"The fault is mine alone; I could not live without him,
 Oh, pardon the Count Nillo, pardon your only child!"

"Silence, dishonored daughter, let me not see your shame,
 Before the morning lightens, the Count shall lose his head."
"Let the headsman be prepared to take my life likewise,
 And the sexton dig a grave wide for a double bed."

The mournful bells are ringing; for whose death do they knell?
 Count Nillo has been slain; the Infanta's soul has flown;
The body of Count Nillo was buried in the porch,
 The Infanta laid to rest before the altar throne.

A cypress and an orange sprang from these lovers' graves,
 They grew and leaned together, and with their branches kissed.
The King in savage anger bade axemen cut them down,
 But from their severed trunks arose a heavenly mist.

From his cloud came a pigeon, from her cloud a ringdove,
 They flew before the King at his table as he ate.
"Accursed be the loves that thus mock me to my face,
 And neither life nor death has power to separate."

HUNGARIAN FOLK-SONGS.

THERE is a Hungarian proverb which says, "The Magyar amuses himself by weeping." There is an underlying element of melancholy in this proud and high-spirited race, and its susceptibility to sadness is manifest in its folk-poetry as in its remarkable and powerful national music, which has for the fine ear a note of lamentation beneath its fiery tone. This is not singular, for the folk-songs of almost every nation have this pervading element to a greater or less degree, characterized by shades of temperament and national and historical influences, and showing that the minds of primitive peoples were most deeply affected by the woes of life rather than its joys, and the disappointments rather than the successes of passion, which express themselves in poetry. The aspects of nature, particularly the loneliness of vast plains such as exist in Hungary, and the enforced pensiveness of the shepherd life, exercise a powerful influence in giving a melancholy tinge to popular poetry, and in its melody and in its thought it breathes the note of the rain-laden breeze that sighs across the vast expanse, and the lights of whose magic sunshine are rather of sadness than exhilaration. Like all primitive poetry, born in times of strife and a disorganized and turbulent condition of society, the Magyar ballads deal with violent passions and bloodshed, and the brigands, who were rather military outlaws than common robbers, are the popular heroes, and appeal to the peasant imagination as the embodiments of the revolt of the people against the tyranny of the rich and powerful. But, in spite of their exploits, the gallows always waits for them, and the ballads end with the dismal spectacle of the body swinging in the wind on the deadly tree, while in the midst of their carousings the note of sadness and the foreboding of certain fate constantly intrudes. The Magyar brigand ballads have a much deeper element of poetry and passion than is to be found in the coarse humor and vulgar trickery of the English Robin Hood ballads, and express a finer and more delicate fibre of national feeling. The prevalent characteristics of Magyar folk-poetry are, however, the same as those of the higher standard of popular ballads, and were produced by similar influences, and in similar condition of mind. There is the same vigor of expression and strength of natural imagery, the same abruptness and disconnection in the construction in which dramatic dialogue is interjected into description with a perfect faith in the hearer's comprehension, the same naïveté and freshness of language, and the same simplicity and passion of thought. Those striking coincidences in subject and form of expression which are noted, to the wonder and bewilderment of the students of folk-poetry and folk-tales, in the most widely diverse nations, and which would almost lead to the belief in a common origin and derivation, or to some means of intercommunication yet unknown, are to be found in the Magyar ballads, connecting them with the common stock. In the specimens which follow, the ballad of Poisoned Janos is almost exactly similar in construction and refrain to the Scotch ballad of Lord Randal: —

"O, where hae ye been, Lord Randal, my son,
  O, where hae ye been, my handsome young man?"
"I hae been to the wild-wood; mother, make my bed soon,
  For I'm wearie wi hunting, and fain wald lie down!" —

with the substitution of the "crab with four feet" for the "eels boiled in broo"—the conventional poisoned dish. The same ballad in substance and form of expression, with the same devising of property to friends and the same bestowal of a curse upon the murderess, is to be found in Danish, German, Dutch, Swedish, Spanish, Italian, and other European folk-poetry, and may yet be discovered in Africa and the South Seas. The circumstance of the infant speaking from the cradle, giving warning of the faithlessness of his mother in Barcsai is common in the folk-ballads of many nations, and the incident of a bird's singing ill-news, the request of a dead man for a peculiar kind of coffin and a favorite burial place, and the growing together of flowers from the graves of a loving couple, are almost universal features in popular poetry; and the rejection of the body of a murdered man by a stream is also familiar. The griefs and sorrows over mortality, the laments of disappointed love, the woes of lonely old age, the remorse for sin, and the fierce passions of jealousy and revenge are common to human nature, and are interpreted in the same language the world over, whether in civilization or barbarism.

In regard to the versions which follow, it is needless to state the difficulty of transferring the original vividness of expression, or preserving the effect of the repetitions and other peculiarities of primitive poetry in the conventional fetters of modern verse and rhyme. The first ballad, Barcsai, is given in a literal translation in order that these forms and turns of expression may be appreciated. The others have been rendered as literally and with as much of the original flavor as possible, but with a consciousness that much of the latter has inevitably evaporated. As says M. Jean de Nathy, to whose literal translations into French, Ballades et Chansons Populaires de la Hongrie, I am indebted for my knowledge of Magyar folk-poetry: "For the greater part without rhymes, they abound in repetition of words and parts of phrases, in alliterations and parallelism, called by the poet Arany 'rhymes of thought,' which are difficult to render in modern forms of verse."

BARCSAI.

"Go, my master, go to Kolozvar,
To Kolozvar, to the mansion of my father,
And bring me, bring me the great piece of linen,
The great piece of linen, of linen fine that I have had as a
    present."

"Do not go, my father, do not go, do not quit your mansion,
For my lady mother, in truth, loves Barcsai."

"Hearest thou, wife, hearest thou what says the infant?"
"Do not believe him, my dear master, the infant is drunken."

He is gone upon the words of his wife,
Upon the words of his wife toward Kolozvar.
Before he had traveled half of the road,
There came to his spirit the words of the little infant,
And immediately he returns toward the mansion,
Toward the mansion. Before his door he halts.

"Open the door, open the door, my lady wife."
"In a moment I will open it, in a moment, my dear, beloved
    master,

But first let me put on my every-day garment,
But first let me put on my apron."

"Open the door, open the door, my lady wife."
"In a moment I will open it, my dear beloved master,
But first let me put on my shoes new-soled,
But first let me knot around my head my every-day kerchief."

"Open the door, open the door, my lady wife."
She did not know what to say; to open the door she was
    forced.

"Give me, give me, the key to the great chest."
"I cannot give you it, I cannot give you the key of the great
    chest,
In the neighborhood I have been; I jumped over the hedge,
And it's there I lost the key of the great chest —
We will find it at the fair blush of morning,
At the fair blush of morning, at the brightening of the earth."

Then he struck so strongly the great painted chest
That he broke it in two halves.
Barcsai fell out and rolled upon the earth.
He took his sword and cut off his head.

"Hearken, my wife, hearken, my wife, hearken,
Of three deaths, which do you choose?
Do you choose that I cut off your head?
Or with your silky locks that I sweep the house?

Or do you choose to watch until the morning,
And serve as a torch to seven wassailers?"
"Of the three deaths I choose
To serve as a torch to seven wassailers."

"My servant, my servant, my very little servant,
Bring me, bring the great pot of pitch.
Bring me, bring me, the great piece of linen,
The great piece of linen, of linen fine, received as a present.
Begin at her head, and to the sole of her feet wrap her,
The fine linen knot around her head.
Begin at her head, and to the sole of her feet cover her with
    pitch.
Begin at the sole of her feet and set the whole on fire.

"At her head I will place the Wallach fifer,
At her feet I will place the gypsy fiddler.
Whistle, Wallach, whistle from thy Wallach pipe,
Play, gypsy, play from thy gypsy fiddle,
Whistle with all thy might, play with all thy soul,
That the heart of my wife may be rejoiced."

KURIS PISTA.

"Go, my child, where the maidens spin
    Within their chamber fair."
"Ah, mother, I dare not venture in,
    For Kuris will be there."

"If he be there, you need not fear,
    The young men will thee guard."
The judge's daughter, with glances clear,
    Sits in the young men's ward.

Kuris Pista, indeed, was there,
    And to the girl drew nigh,
His words he spoke with gracious air,
    "The gay dance let us try."

"Oh, let me go, or I shall fall,
    And in this place will die."
But Kuris heeded not her call,
    And fire lit in his eye.

"Play, gypsy, play more loud and fast,
    Play till your tight strings break.
Though feet may fail, the dance shall last
    For the mad music's sake."

"Oh, let me go! Oh, let me go!
    My treasure, let me loose,
The red blood from my heart does flow,
    And fills my soaking shoes."

"I will not loose you till you die,
    My treasure and my dove.
Not once but twelve times o'er have I
    Been spurned in asking love."

   · · · · · ·

"Oh, mother, open wide the gate,
    Of your leaved garden thick,
The young men with a litter wait,
    Bearing thy daughter sick.

"Oh, mother, open wide the gate,
    Of your rose garden red,
The young men with a litter wait,
    Bearing thy daughter dead."

Oh, sorrow has her father dear,
    The mother a heartbreak.
They did not heed their daughter's fear
    Her lover's rage to wake.

"Since you would not be mine,
　No other shall you wed.
My blood shall flow with thine,
　One mingled streamlet red.
Our bodies side by side
　In one tomb close shall lie,
To God, the glorified
　Our souls together fly."

THE MURDERED YOUTH.

They have killed the gallant youth,
　For his sixty florins white,
In the Tizta they have thrown him,
　For his stallion bay and bright.

The Tizta would not keep him
　In its waves nor let him float,
On the strand a fisher found him
　And took him into his boat.

His mother came to wake him,
　But her voice he could not hear,
"Rise up, rise up, my gallant son,
　Your mother's heart is here."

His father came to wake him,
　But his voice he could not hear,
"Rise up, rise up, my gallant son,
　Your father's house is near."

His sweetheart came to wake him,
　But her voice he could not hear,

"Rise up, rise up, my rosemary,
  Clasp my neck with arms so dear."

"Oh, tell me, will you make me
  A coffin of walnut bright?"
"My darling, I will make you
  A coffin of marble white."

"Oh, tell me, will you robe me
  In a shroud of lawn's fine stitch?"
"My darling, I will robe you
  In a shroud of velvet rich."

"Oh, tell me, if my coffin new
  You'll trim with nails of brass?"
"My darling, on your coffin new
  Gold nails shall be thick as grass."

"Oh, tell me, will you lay me
  In the graveyard's grassy glade?"
"My darling, I will lay you
  In my own rose garden's shade."

"Oh, tell me, will you mourn me,
  With three maids to see your tears?"
"My darling, I will mourn you
  Until all the wide world hears."

THE THREE BRIGANDS.

Always ranging night and day,
  The three brigands bold
Are seeking their prey,
  In the forest old.

In the forest old they meet a Greek,
  And the Greek they slay,
From his full wagon
  Bear booty away.

Always ranging on the way,
  The three brigands bold
Reach a roadside tavern's
  Sheltering fold.
One cries aloud, "Ho, landlady gay,
  Bring in your good wine."
"My daughter shall serve,
  And I too am fine."

They eat and drink,
  The three brigands bold,
But the youngest thief
  Sits pallid and cold,
To himself he says, "My cradle should
  A coffin have made.
My infant linen
  For a shroud been laid,
And my swaddling cord
  My body swayed."

THE BELLS OF TARJA.

From bells of Tarja the sad notes flow:
  Faded the sweetheart of the brave youth.
Three doves are ringing the bells of woe,
  To mourn their sister in love and truth.

With lily flowers they painted her shroud,
  And that is why 't is so pure and white.

Her love bends o'er it, and weeps aloud ;
   His heart's black tears its radiance blight.

They planted rosemary on her grave ;
   Weeping he followed his sweetheart's hearse.
His tears were dew where grave grasses wave :
   "Return my love or have my curse !"

Her linen chemise none will wash now,
   Except the rain of his weeping eyes ;
The tangled curls on her pallid brow
   No one will caress with soothing sighs.

Again at Tarja the bells ring slow —
   For the youth himself they sadly toll.
He wept so much for his dove laid low,
   To-day they weep his own parting soul.

Young maids, young maids of Tarja's plum grove,
   By constant presence pay love's debts.
For a young man's heart breaks for his dove,
   While a young girl's heart weeps and forgets.

THE BETROTHED.

"In the great court of thy small dwelling,
   My dear rose, what doest thou ? "
"I cook my pullets ; my heart I 'm telling
   My love for his supper will come but now."

"In the great court of thy small dwelling,
   My dear rose, what doest thou ? "
"I trim my dress ; my heart I 'm telling
   My love will be coming with shining brow."

"In the great court of thy small dwelling,
    My dear rose, what doest thou?"
"I gather flowers; my heart I'm telling
    My garlanded hair will attest my vow."

"Cook not your fowls, nor trim your dresses,
    Put no flowers in your hair.
My dear rose pale, for your raven tresses
    A branch of willow you may find and wear."

The fatal fight is done and over,
    Three came back to tell the tale.
On the bloody field there lies thy lover,
    And his winding sheet is his broken mail.

"Oh, cruel bird, I'll curse your singing,
    Fatal voice that tears my breast.
My mother the shroud will soon be bringing,
    And in white grave clothes I'll be drest."

POISONED JANOS.

"Whence comest thou with knitted brows,
    My heart, my soul, my little son?"
"I come from my love's sister's house,
    Dear lady mother.
    Oh, my heart aches so,
    Make ready my bed."

"What has she given you to eat,
    My heart, my soul, my little son?"
"She gave me a crab with four feet,[1]

---

[1] The crab with four feet is the conventional poisonous food in Hungarian folk-lore, as the toad is in English and the spotted frog in French.

Dear lady mother.
Oh, my heart aches so,
Make ready my bed."

"How served she it for you to dine,
My heart, my soul, my little son?"
"She served it in a salver fine,
Dear lady mother.
Oh, my heart aches so,
Make ready my bed."

"Is it that makes you look so white,
My heart, my soul, my little son?"
"Yes, that will kill me ere the night,
Dear lady mother.
Oh, my heart aches so,
Make ready my bed."

"What will you leave your father gray,
My heart, my soul, my little son?"
"My brass-trimmed wagon, new and gay,
Dear lady mother.
Oh, my heart aches so,
Make ready my bed."

"What will you leave your brother brave,
My heart, my soul, my little son?"
"My four strong oxen he can have,
Dear lady mother.
Oh, my heart aches so,
Make ready my bed."

"What will you leave your brother fair,
My heart, my soul, my little son?"
"My four swift horses for his share,

Dear lady mother.
Oh, my heart aches so,
Make ready my bed."

"What will you leave your sister bright,
My heart, my soul, my little son?"
"My household vessels silver white,
Dear lady mother.
Oh, my heart aches so,
Make ready my bed."

"What will you leave your love's false kin,
My heart, my soul, my little son?"
"The fire of hell her heart within,
Dear lady mother.
Oh, my heart aches so,
Make ready my bed."

"What will you leave your mother dear,
My heart, my soul, my little son?"
"The grief and pain you'll have to bear,
Dear lady mother.
Oh, my heart aches so,
Make ready my bed."

GYURI BANDI.

The rain falls in a few small drops,
　Gyuri Bandi beside the gallows cries,
Beyond Szeged the woodman chops
　The tree, from which the croaking raven flies.

Yet Gyuri Bandi naught has done
　But twist his kerchief to a solid cord,

And knot it round his wife's neck bone,
  To deck a tree for her sovereign lord.

His shirt and kilt he'd bade her lave,
  That he might ride to his captain's abode. —
Then he bridled his steed so brave,
  And away to his rose's bower he rode.

"Ah, mother dear, I have sinned a sin,
  I've killed my wife with my love to go." —
Then Gyuri Bandi drank at the inn,
  And slept in the cloak of Kasa his foe.

Gyuri Bandi was bound with chains,
  From the judge's mouth his doom was told,
The gallows tree in winds and rains
  Dandles and rocks him, alone and cold.

Gyuri Bandi had never thought
  The wind would rock him on the gallows tree,
Even Kasa himself, whose blood he'd sought,
  Was dismal at heart the sad sight to see.

THE MOTHER AND DAUGHTER.

"Soft shines the light of the evening star,
  Beneath my window my love stands tall.
Dear mother, let me undo the bar,
  My heart beats fast to come at his call."

"My darling rose, to the window glide,
  Your honey lips let me deeply kiss,
A thousand sorrows in my heart abide,
  With but a touch they'll bloom in bliss."

"Mother, do you hear his magic call?
    I have tied a bunch of roses red,
In his hat to shine above them all,
    As pride of his kiss would lift my head."

"My daughter, you are too young for love,
    Too soon it is for the matron's cap,
For a maiden's smile the world will move,
    With lover's tears for joy's good hap."

"Dearest rose, to each other we're due,
    We'll marry the coming Easter morn,
Believe me, I'll be more kind to you
    Than both your parents since you were born.

"Mother, do you hear my lover's vow,
    Believe me, my pearl will be my life.
Dear mother, let me go to him now,
    I die to tell him I'll be his wife."

"My darling, don't trust to young men's speech,
    He'll love you while you are not his own,
But marriage its sorry lore will teach,
    With a cudgel's blow to make you groan."

"I have seen my father beat you too,
    But for all his blows you love him dear;
I'm sure I can love as well as you,
    And no warning voice shall make me fear."

THE THREE ORPHANS.

"Where go ye, dear orphans three?"
    "Far from this place for work to seek."

"Oh, do not go, dear orphans three,
    For work you are too small and weak."

"Come, I will give you three small wands,
    Upon your mother's grave to knock."
"Arise, arise, our mother dear,
    Cold and ragged are your flock."

"I cannot rise, dear orphans three,
    Within my shroud I'm dried to bone;
But you have now a second mother,
    Who will tend you as her own."

"When she combs our tangled hair,
    Her talons scratch and make us bleed,
And when she gives us food to eat,
    'Tis with curses she would feed."

BUGA JAKAB.

"Why do you grumble, comrade, that there's nothing in your purse?
  God is good, his gifts are sure, keep up your heart from woe;
The winter it will soon be past, the bloom come to the furze,
  And where our eyes look round us we will go."

"How can I help my sadness, lad, how can I drop my care?
  All the ills of life I feel in my bosom sore;
I cannot sleep nor rest, nor breathe refreshing air,
  My heart is in a well and covered o'er.

"My side is naked to the blast, my coat to rags is torn,
  My shoulder blade is bleeding raw, where my belt will chafe,

My horse has lost a shoe behind, the others they are worn,
  And I 'm afraid that none of them are safe.

" In my mantle the rain has soaked, and rotted its strength
      away,
  I cannot hope for another ; no one will make a gift ;
I have my wallet still, but bare and empty it must stay ;
  But that is not the worst of all my shrift.

" From my trimming of good wolf's fur the hair is falling out,
  Across my flagon's mouth the spider has spun a sheet ;
The joys of youth have left me ; no one comes me about,
  To wash my sweated shirt and make it neat."

" For all the ills of life, my friend, one lives as best one may.
  The blest rays of the sunshine still warm my heart and
      breast.
When I can't eat, I light my pipe, and puff my care away.
  Poor fellows live ; I live as do the rest."

THE FAIR ILONA.

" Heaven bless you,
    Judge, my lord,
  Keep your house
    In safe accord."

" What kind fortune
    Did you send
  To my house
    Your steps to bend ? "

" I led my geese
    To meadows green,

>   The judge's son
>   With stones was seen,
>   He killed my gosling
>   Of yellow sheen."

"What shall be paid,
    Ilona fair,
For thy young gosling
    The lad killed there?"

"For each of his feathers,
    A ducat bright;
For each of his feet,
    A spoon so white;
For his two wings
    Two salvers dight;
For his warbling throat
    A horn of might."

"If your demands
    You place so high,
Upon the gallows
    The lad must die."

"May the gallows tree
    Be a rose, my lord,
And my two arms
    Its strangling cord."

THE BRIGAND'S WIFE.

Often my father and mother I prayed
    Not to send me up to the mountain high,

To the mountain cold, where the brigand strayed,
    And waited to clutch me as I came nigh.

At this very hour at the highway cross,
    He waits for the stranger to rob his gold,
The robbed has only his money's loss,
    But the wretched robber his soul has sold.

In the morn I rise bloody clothes to lave,
    In the early morn, where the stream runs still.
"Why weepest thou, girl?" "No sorrows I have,
    But my fire's sharp smoke has made my eyes fill."

THE GIRL AND THE SHEPHERD.

The night sinks softly on the plain,
    The heifer's bell is still;
A lone pipe calls with magic strain—
    The girl leans on the sill.

"Here on the prairie I am alone;
    My cows and horses rest;"
The young girl to the plain has gone
    With longing in her breast.

The master's herd is moving slow;
    The young girl follows on;
"Dear shepherd, spread your soft cloak now
    The dewy earth upon."

The wheat has not filled out its ear,
    But birds have picked the grain;
"See, mother, in the early year,
    How love has brought me pain."

"My daughter, I will curse your name,
   If you the shepherd wed."
"Mother, I'll bear your fiercest blame,
   My heart will rest his head."

THE THREE SCARFS.

I've bought three scarfs of white;
   I'll be white as any swan,
And none will dare embrace me,
   When the three white scarfs I don.

I've bought three scarfs of red;
   I'll be red as any rose;
My love will rain his kisses
   When such a floweret blows.

I've bought three scarfs of gold;
   I'll be yellow as its hue;
I'll glitter like a weathercock,
   While all the world shines new.

I've bought three scarfs of brown;
   I'll be brown as any owl;
None will dare to ask a kiss
   From such a timorous fowl.

THE LOVELIEST FLOWER OF ALL.

In the harvest field there are three flowers.
   These words said the bright flower of corn:
I am the brightest that charms the hours,
I'm gathered for the church, and they say I'm the flesh of
   Christ new born.

In the harvest field there are three flowers,
   These words said the flower of the vine:
I am the brightest in all the bowers,
I'm gathered for the church, and they say the red blood of
    Christ is mine.

In the harvest field there are three flowers,
   These words said the wee violet blue:
I am the brightest beneath the showers,
For the young maidens cull me to deck the hats of those they
    love so true.

THE LONESOME ONE.

Before thy door the bright, green corn
   Bends o'er the pebbly path,
Its blooming flowers are not yet born —
   Two doves coo in the math.

Comes tripping by a village lass:
   Her skirts are wet with dew,
Has she been raking the moistened grass?
   Oh, I am far from you.

My sweetheart, I'm as far from you
   As I have been for years,
Of her I ask each stranger new,
   No tidings reach my ears.

O'er the lone prairie the wind whistles cold,
   The young shepherd sadly follows his way.

"Where is your flock?" "Oh, my sheep I have sold."
   "Where is your gayety?" "Vanished away."

"Your sheep you have sold! Why did you so?"
   "Because on earth I shall need nothing more."
"Why did your light heart to a sad one grow?"
   "Because my false love has wounded it sore."

"God guard you, dear prairie, and comrades brave,
   My reed pipe again I shall never play."
O'er the lone prairie the bitter winds rave,
   The young shepherd sadly follows his way.

   May beetle, golden beetle;
     I do not ask when summer will come;
   I do not ask how long I shall live,
     I only ask for my rose in bloom.

   May beetle, golden beetle;
     I do not ask for the summer's light,
   For a summer's fire in my heart has burned,
     Since my rose first flamed upon my sight.

The time will come, the time will come,
   When you will come to weep before the house;
When you will clasp the doorpost of the entrance,
   In deep regret for your unfaithful vows.

The time will come, the time will come,
   When you will come to weep before my door.
Perhaps I may a word or two say to you,
   But not the words I said to you before.

When I was a gallant lad,
    I'd come from my door with glee;
I'd thrill the air with shouts of joy,
    And the world would know 't was me.

Now I am a graybeard old,
    I come from my door with pain,
Let me shout as loud as I may,
    No voice will answer again.

The petals of the white rose fall;
    To-day another weds my rose.
Through the wood the violins call,
    And my heart shuts tight with its woes.

The shining star adorns the night,
    In vain for thee my heart has beat,
My star for me has quenched its light,
    But in my heart its ray is sweet.

At Dobreesen flowers a fair rose-tree;
    It bears a lovely perfumed rose,
But what is that lovely rose worth to me,
    If far beyond my reach it blows.

The young postilion is sounding his horn,
    He brings a letter from my dear.
But her letter of gold leaves me forlorn,
    Since she comes not to meet me here.

Down there under the steep hillside,
    A small apple-tree blooms in pride.

Its flowers are **fair**; its fruit is sweet,
A little maiden sits at its feet.

She tresses garlands of red and white;
On her breast they turn to silver bright.

She lifts her eyes to the heavens vast,
And sees a wide road winding past.

Its borders two like silver gleam,
The middle is a golden stream.

A lamb walks there with curly bell,
On each curl point tinkles a bell.

The wild duck broods in the reedy grass,
  In the meadow rich ripens the corn,
But the place where lives a faithful lass
  I never have found since I was born.

In the lonesome night the stars are **falling**,
  The young man drags his feet toward the house.
Heavy in his heart are voices calling,
  And hatred of the world his miseries arouse.

In the lonesome night the stars are falling,
  In the white mansion the candle glimmers red.
Flowers strew the couch. Oh, the sight appalling!
  The brown girl in her shroud lies stretched upon her bed.

They are sweeping the wide street.
    The soldiers start marching down;
A maid of sixteen, red and sweet,
    Is following out of town.

The young captain turns and speaks:
    "What this means I must know."
She answers with tear-wet cheeks,
    "I follow where'er you go."

The roads are thick with snow,
    The black steed gallops wide.
His bridle reins hang low
    In his mad master's ride.

The brigand on the steed
    Breathes deep, and sadly sighs,
"I dreamed not, in my need,
    She'd sell me to the spies.

"Of all the brigands cursed,
    Who rob on the wide plain,
The soldiers seek me first,
    To bind me with a chain.

"My father was a thief,
    My grandfather likewise.
To honest life's relief,
    How can such seed arise?"

FOLK-SONGS OF ROUMANIA.

It gives one a strange idea of what treasures of primitive poetry and music may yet be found among the peasantry of Europe, when a volume like this — The Bard of the Dimbovitza, Roumanian Folk-Songs. Collected from the Peasants by Helene Vacaresco. Translated by Carmen Sylva and Alma Strettell — has been brought to light from the single district of Roumania. The preface by Carmen Sylva (the Queen of Roumania), herself an accomplished literary artist, says that these songs were collected from the lips of peasant girls, the lute players, the reapers, and the gypsies, by the young poetess Helene Vacaresco, in the district of Roumania, in which her father's domain is situated. She spent four years in collecting them, and even although her family has been known and honored for centuries by the people, she encountered many difficulties in endeavoring to induce the peasants to repeat their songs to her. "She was forced to affect a desire to learn spinning that she might join the girls at their spinning parties, and so overhear their songs more easily;

she hid in the tall maize to hear the reapers crooning; she caught them from the lips of peasant women, of lute players ('Cobzars,' so called from the name of their instrument, the cobza, or lute), of gypsies, of fortune tellers; she listened for them by death-beds, by cradles, at the dance, and in the tavern with inexhaustible patience." The result is a volume which is not only equal in quality to that of the finest folk-song and poetry which any European nation possesses, and with a peculiar and original flavor of its own, revealing strong and original national characteristics, but, one is tempted to say, with more of the sublimated and naked essence of poetry than can be found in any work of modern civilized poets. There are times when the vivid strength of simple passions, expressed with the force of naked directness without any weakening refinement of language, the feelings of a people to whom love is a genuine and undisguised passion, in whom hatred burns the blood and finds relief in the shot or the stab, to whom death is an object of vital horror as the end of life and happiness, and to whom religion is an embodiment of direct supernatural power, produce a poetry, which reaches a force of expression and touches the heart with a power to which all modern refinements of thought and language are unable to attain. It is, in comparison, as if a cloud of unreality, the emanations of artificial thoughts and sentiments, or the dust, as it were, of ages, had fallen upon the native freshness of feeling and language, and that civilized men were no longer able to feel so deeply or to speak so clearly as those who had never been burdened with knowledge, or the strength of whose emotions had not been diluted by the restraints and refinements of civilization, transcendental religion, or artificial society. There is, of course, a power and subtlety of thought in minds which have inherited the world's wisdom and knowledge, and their thoughts have a scope and extent to which those of unlettered peasants are strangers, and their views of the problems of life and humanity are as those of a man to a child; but the strength of their feeling in simple passion is much diluted and their powers of expression are correspondingly less, so far as vividness and simplicity are concerned. As an illustration of the weakness of purely artistic literature, whatever its beauty and skill, to touch the depths of feeling like the purely unsophisticated language of the natural poets, who simply endeavored to express their emotions without thought of form or artistic melody, may be compared the closing aspiration of the famous and beautiful serenade in Maud, —

    She is coming, my own, my sweet;
      Were it ever so airy a tread,
    My heart would hear her and beat,

> Were it earth in an earthy bed;
> My dust would hear her and beat,
> Had I lain for a century dead;
> Would start and tremble under her feet,
> And blossom in purple and red, —

with the simple utterance of the Javanese lover in one of the natural flowers of folk-song, —

> I do not know when I shall die,
> I have seen at Badoer many that were dead,
> They were dressed in white shrouds, and
> Were buried in the earth;
> If I die at Badoer and am buried beyond the
> Village eastward against the hill,
> Where the grass is high,
> Then will Adinda pass by there, and the border
> Of her sarong will sweep softly along the grass, —
> I shall hear it.

There are times when the vitality of poetry seems to be lost as one feels the simple and direct power of some of these ancient songs which spring from the heart and not from the head, and all modern verse seems like the pale and artificial product of intellectuality, weakened feeling, and language refined until it has lost its strength, and one is almost tempted to believe that civilization is as fatal to poetry as it is to religious enthusiasm. Of course this is not the case. The human heart has not lost its strength of feeling nor its power of expression, and modern poetry is greater in its power and wider in its scope than folk-song. But it has lost some of the peculiar strength which comes from simplicity of feeling and overmastering power of passion; and its language, if it has many delicate shades of meaning, which that of a primitive people has not, has lost the clearness and vividness of expression of those whose words are few, but which are the creation of their hearts and not of their intellects.

These folk-songs of Roumania are full of the pathos and strength of simple passions, and they show a native poetical spirit and power of the imagination which is rare in any nation. Doubtless many of them are old, the inheritance of long tradition and familiar forms of expression, but it is indicated that many of them are new, and that the stock is being constantly added to by the force of a poetic inspiration, which is still in full life and flower. We are told that many of the spinning songs are improvisations, the girls all standing in a circle, the best spinner or singer in the centre, and that she begins to improvise a song, which is passed on for continuance with the distaff to any one whom she may select. Doubtless these are on familiar themes and with familiar forms of expression, like all folk-songs, but they show the vital spirit of poetry still existing, and the bulk of more elaborate compositions is probably still being added to. This fact confirms the belief, which intelligent observers have noted, that the Roumanians and the kindred peoples of this race have an intellectual power which is of an undecayed and still progressive people, very different from the effete Ottomans by whom they were so long oppressed, and that, if the future promised an opportunity for original development, instead of absorption into the Muscovite empire, they might produce a homogeneous and progressive nation with original features and an independent contribution to civilization. At any rate the volume gives evidence of remarkable intellectual power among the Roumanian peasantry, and it may be hoped that this treasure-trove will stimulate other researches, and the discovery of a larger bulk of native poetry, if none of finer value. Whether any touch of sentiment has been added in the translations with the higher poetic form in some instances cannot, of course, be apparent, but the internal evidence would indicate that essential faithfulness has been preserved and that the substance is as genuine as the poetry is original and powerful.

Some of the most striking songs in the collection are those of the gypsies, which have a wild and fiery tone like the gypsy music which has stirred the blood of refined civilization, as it has been performed by orchestras with all the effect of modern instrumentation, in a way that the most skillful composers have failed to do, and shows the element of poetry and passion in that strange and exotic race. What stronger beauty of expression or grace of feeling can be found than this? —

> There where the path to the plain goes by,
> Where deep in the thicket my hut doth lie,
> Where corn stands green in the garden plot —
> The brook ripples by so clearly there,
> The way is so open, so white, and fair —
> My heart's best beloved, he takes it not.
>
> There where I sit by my door and spin,
> While morning winds that blow out and in
> With scent of roses enfold the spot,
> When at evening I softly sing my lay,
> That the wand'rer hears, as he goes his way —
> My heart's best beloved, he hears it not.
>
> There, where on Sunday I go alone
> To the old, old well with the milk-white stone,
> Where by the fence, in a nook forgot,
> Rises a spring in the daisied grass,
> That makes whoso drink of it love — alas!
> My heart's best beloved, he drinks it not.
>
> There, by my window, where day by day,
> When the sunbeams first brighten the morning gray,
> I lean and dream of my weary lot,
> And wait his coming, and softly cry
> Because of love's longing that makes one die —
> My heart's best beloved, he dieth not.

A peculiar character in the Roumanian songs is that of the Heiduck, a sort of combination, it would seem, of the knight-errant and the brigand, with all the legendary attributes of beauty, strength, courage, and generosity of the half-fabulous popular heroes of all nations. The Song of the Heiduck has all the buoyant spirit and gayety appropriate to such a figure, but is overshadowed also by a sort of elfin sadness and the doom of a supernatural fate, which is chiefly to be found in those nations which have a tinge of oriental mysticism, and is a marked feature of the Roumanian folk-songs. The Celtic mysticism, where it exists, is more strictly religious.

THE HEIDUCK'S SONG.

I tell the forest the wonders I see in my dreams
And the forest loves to hear the tale of my dreaming
  More than the song of birds,
  More than the murmur of leaves.

The huts had well-nigh beguiled me to stay, for the windows
Stood wide, and the smiles of the maidens shone out from
    within,
But the Heiduck am I — and I love the far-stretching roads
    And the plain, and my galloping steed.
My mother gave birth to me, sure, on a sunshiny morning,
And had I but never known love, ah, how happy were I!
I sing at the hour when the moon climbs above the horizon;
The tales that the aged folk know, I can tell, every one,

And I make the young dance, when I sing, to the tune of
    my ballads.
    For I a strange woman have loved;
She comes every night to me now, and she kisses my forehead,
    And asks if I love her still.
    She carries a knife in her girdle — her eyes have a glitter
    Like daggers — her hand is as white as the veil of a bride;
But her voice I have never heard — yet know I full surely,
    She asks if I love her still.
In token thereof I have given her up my girdle,
    My cap with its feathers gay,
My mantle with broid'ry brave, and my glitt'ring daggers.
And my songs, I have given them all to her, one by one,
Yet the gayest bring no smile to her face, and the saddest
    Are powerless to make her sad.
Then hence she goes, by the small plank over the river
    The plank that sways to her step.
The willows bow down their heads, and bend as she passes . . .
    And morning cometh, and findeth me poor and trembling,
Since she hath taken my all from me, even my songs.
Yet is she not content, nor will cease from asking,
    Whether I love her still.

I tell the forest the wonders I see in my dreams
And the forest loves to hear the tale of my dreaming,
    More than the song of birds,
    More than the murmur of leaves.

Almost all the songs have the refrain, as in this example, which is not, necessarily, directly associated with the subject of the song, but is suggested by some incident, circumstance, or scene brought to the mind at the time of the recital. As often in the old Scotch ballads, it adds a weird and touching effect like a dominant note in music, or a symbolical background to a picture.

A marked feature in these folk-songs of Roumania, as in those of all other nations, is the place which fighting has in them, the songs of the soldiers who are going to battle for their native land, and the emotions of heroism, courage, and self-devotion; but as in all these songs there is an underlying element of melancholy, mysticism, and refined and delicate feeling, quite different from the savage ferocity, heartiness, and humor of more northern nations, and there is no trace whatever of the farcical rudeness and cunning which is attached to some of the heroes of the Scandinavian ballads. The sentiments expressed are those of singular refinement for a primitive people, and the general tone of the soldier songs is one of sadness and content in death, rather than of the fierce joy and hope of the conflict, as in the following characteristic specimen:—

"I AM CONTENT."

A spindle of hazel-wood had I;
Into the mill-stream it fell one day
The water has brought it me back no more.

As he lay a-dying the soldier spake —
"I am content.

Let my mother be told in the village there,
  And my bride in the hut be told,
    That they must pray with folded hands,
      With folded hands for me."
The soldier is dead — and with folded hands,
  His bride and his mother pray.
On the field of battle they dug his grave,
And red with his life-blood the earth was dyed,
  The earth they laid him in.
The sun looked down on him there and spake,
  "I am content."
And flowers bloomed thickly upon his grave,
  And were glad they blossomed there.

And when the wind in the treetops roared,
The soldier asked from the deep, dark grave,
  "Did the banner flutter then?"
"Not so, my hero," the wind replied,
"The fight is done, but the banner won,
  Thy comrades of old have borne it hence,
    Have borne it in triumph hence."
Then the soldier spake from the deep, dark grave:
  "I am content."
And again he heard the shepherds pass,
  And the flocks go wand'ring by,
And the soldier asked, "Is the sound I hear,
  The sound of the battle's roar?"
And they all replied: "My hero, nay!
Thou art dead, and the fight is o'er,
  Our country joyful and free."
Then the soldier spake from the deep, dark grave:
  "I am content."

Then he heareth the lovers laughing pass,
And the soldier asks once more:
"Are these not the voices of them that love,
That love and remember me?"
"Not so, my hero," the lovers say:
"We are those that remember not;
For the spring has come and the earth has smiled,
And the dead must be forgot."
Then the soldier spake from the deep, dark grave:
"I am content."

*A spindle of hazel-wood had I;
Into the mill-stream it fell one day,—
The water has brought it me back no more.*

As has been said, the underlying and predominant element of these Roumanian folk-songs is melancholy, and rarely, if ever, in those of any nation, is the sorrow of death and parting more vividly and powerfully expressed. The voices speak from beyond the grave, but they seem to intensify rather than lighten the grief, and the calm and beauty of nature bring no consolation to the stricken heart, but only deepen the agony. This dirge for a child will speak to every one who has known anguish, as with the voice of the wailing wind:—

The river went weeping, weeping,
Ah, me, how it did weep!
But I would never heed it,
The weeping of the river,

  Whilst thou were at my breast.
  The stars — poor stars — were weeping,
  But I would not hear their weeping,
  Whilst yet I heard thy voice.
Unhappy men drew nigh, and told me of their woe,
They said: "We are the sorrow of all humanity."
But I had no compassion for human misery,
  Whilst thou wert with me still.

  Then these, the river with its weeping,
  The piteous stars, the miserable men,
All prayed the earth's dark depths to take thee from me,
That so my woe might understand their woe;
  And now — I weep.
  Yet weep I not for human misery,
  Nor for the stars' complaining,
  Nor for the river's wailing.
  I weep for thee alone, most miserly,
  Keep all my tears for thee!
Now I must rock forever empty arms,
That grieve they have no burden any more.
Now I must sing, and know, the while, no ears
  Are there to hearken.

The birds will ask me, "To whom singest thou?"
The moon look down and ask, "Whom rockest thou?"
The grave will be right proud, while I am cursed,
  That I did give her thee.
My womb upbraideth me because I gave
To Death the gift that once she gave to me,
  The gift that sprung from her.
Now must I see thy sleep and never know
  Whether this sleep be sweet.

Then do I ask of Earth
"Is the sleep sweet indeed
That in thy lap we sleep?"
But, ah! thou knowest Earth misliketh pity,
And loves to hold her peace!

Wilt thou then answer in her stead, and say,
"What do the birds, O mother,
Since I have gone to sleep?
And the river with its pebbles,
Since I have gone to sleep?
And thy broken heart, O mother,
Thy little heart, dear mother,
Since I have gone to sleep!
Does my father guide the oxen
Walking beside the ploughshare.
Since I have gone to sleep?"
Oh, say all this to me!
Answer instead of Earth that knows no pity,
And loves to hold her peace.

The river went weeping, weeping,
Ah, me, how it did weep!
But I would never heed it,
The weeping of the river,
Whilst thou were at my breast.
The stars, poor stars, were weeping,
But I would not hear their weeping,
Whilst yet I heard thy voice.

And this other has a beautiful and touching sentiment:—

The river last night swept the bridge away,
And so we must wade through the river to-day.
The maidens **sing as** *they wade,* **and** *are gay.*

A little sister **the** dead child had,
Since it died little sister **has grown more** glad,
And saith **to** the mother : " **Its own sweet** smile
The one that **is dead unto me did give,**
And all the life that it might not live
Now lives in me." But the mother, the while
Fell a-weeping, and **bowed** her head,
And remembered the child that was **dead.**

The river last night swept the bridge away,
And so we must wade through the river to-day.
The maidens sing as they **wade, and are gay.**

There are other sources of grief than that of simple death, whose sorrow can weep itself away, the tragedies of crime and sin and the agonies of remorse. There is an occasional touch of that ferocity which rejoices in a bloody revenge, as would be natural to a passionate people, and which is manifested in the Song of the Dagger.

> The dagger at my belt that dances
>   Whene'er I dance :
> But when I drink the foaming wine cup,
>   Then it grows sad ;
> For it is thirsty, too, the dagger,
>   It thirsts for blood.

But for the most part the songs which relate to violence and bloodshed are the expressions of the remorse that follows the crime, and with a touch of the prevailing mysticism in the reproach of natural objects. The water refuses to quench the thirst of the murderer, and the trees to give him shelter, and he wanders on an endless way haunted by the voice of his crime. The poem entitled The Outcast expresses this feeling of mysterious remorse and unending and unavailing expiation.

THE OUTCAST.

Go not over the little bridge,
    It is too old.
The trees that have been felled to the earth
And the birds that still would perch upon their boughs,
Must fly very close to earth.

Why do they ask me, " Is it thou ? "
Nay, nay, I know of nothing;
No one has told me aught, yet all are afraid of me,
The stones upon the road shrink from my footsteps,
But I am wearier far than if I had trodden them,
I am always left alone, and yet I hear voices always ;
My sleep is never disturbed, and yet I feel
As though I had never slept.
Know ye why I am weary, so very weary,
That if the grave should say to me, " Lie down
Here in my lap and rest " I would bless the grave ?
It is this : I carry one upon my shoulders,
I carry him onward ever, and feel his hands
About my throat, his breath upon my neck.
It is he that makes my step so heavy,

And drives me wild, too, with the sound of his voice,
It is he that drinks my sleep,
And when I ask him, " Whither shall I take thee
That I may carry thee no more ? "
He points to the horizon.
He is as heavy as a widow's heart.
I know, too, all his thoughts, and his thoughts burn me,
Because he thinks upon my sorrow.
And when we pass some hut, I say,
" Let us linger here awhile, this hut seemeth pleasant to me,"
But he answers, " Never a hut may open its doors to thee,"
And when I ask him, " Friend, art thou not yet weary ? "
He answers, " I ?   I rest in thy weariness,
Refresh myself in thy sweat."
Even on my own hearth
I can never set him down over against me,
He clings to my shoulders always —
I know not even his face.
Then I say to him, " Thou unknown one ! "
And he answers me, " Thou accurst ! "

> Go not over the little bridge,
>   It is too old.
> *The trees that have been felled lie on the earth
> And the birds that still would perch upon their boughs
> Must fly very close to earth.*

One of the peculiar customs of Roumania is that of two girls of different families choosing each other as sisters by affinity, called *suratas*, or " sisters of the cross," a relationship sanctioned by the church, and acting as the tie of blood in relation to family marriages. It is this custom which is alluded to in the charming ballad, which recalls the best of those of Spain on similar subjects, with its delicate feeling and graceful expressions:—

HE THAT TOOK NOTHING.

See how it raineth! and the corn is cut upon the plain,
And I have left my sickle, too, forgotten 'mid the grain.
Now there it lies — ah, woe is me! — beneath the falling rain.

Of all the lads that joined the dance each took some sign
    from me —
One took my girdle, and thou know'st full well which that
    may be,
The one, my sister of the cross, I fashioned with thee.

My chain, sweet sister of the cross, another took; what needs
To tell thee which — the one which hath two strings of
    golden beads.

Another took my flower from me — and which one dost thou
    know?
It is, my sister of the cross, the floweret that doth blow
In autumn days among the grass, where thick the plum-trees
    grow.

But only one took naught away, and know'st thou, sister, who?
He of whom I often spake of thee, when I most silent grew,
He, my little sister of the cross, it is I love so true.

Then quick run after him, he dwells beside the mill-pool deep,
And through his slumbers murmuring on, their watch the
    waters keep,
O happy water, that may sing and lull him in his sleep.

Then quickly run thou after him, my sister, do not stay
To watch the flocks upon the hill, that browse the livelong
    day;
Bring him a girdle, and a chain, yea, and a flower—and
    say:

"I found them hard beside the mill, and all of them are
    thine."
But stay not longer lest thou, too, should'st love him, sister
    mine.

That we may both not have to weep together, oh, beware!
My tears could not love thy tears, not yet my care thy care,
They could not dwell within my hut, nor would be welcome
    there.

See how it raineth! and the corn is cut upon the plain,
And I have left my sickle, too, forgotten 'mid the grain,
Now there it lies — ah, woe to me! beneath the falling rain.

The spinning songs, which are absolutely improvisations, have, of course, all the inevitable character of abruptness and irregularity, but a charming grace of feeling is often visible through them, and their imagery is as effective as it is spontaneous and natural.

SPINNING SONG.

What didst thou, mother, when thou wert a maiden?—
    I was young.—
Didst thou, like me, hark to the moon's soft footfalls,
    Across the sky?
Or didst thou watch the little stars' betrothal?—

Thy father cometh home, leave the door open —

Down to the fountain didst thou go, and there
Thy wooden pitcher filled, didst thou yet linger
Another hour with the full pitcher by thee —
   I was young, —

And did thy tears make glad thy countenance?
And did thy sleep bring gladness to the night?
And did thy dreams bring gladness to thy sleep?
And didst thou smile even by graves, despite
   Thy pity for the dead?

Thy father cometh home, leave the door open

Loved'st thou strawberries and raspberries,
Because they are as red as maidens' lips?
Didst thou love thy girdle for its many pearls,
The river and the wood, because they lie
   So close behind the village?

Didst love the beating of thy heart,
There close beneath thy bodice,
Even though 't were not thy Sunday bodice?

— Thy father cometh home, leave the door open.

These specimens will give an idea of the charm, the grace, the pathos, and the melody of these Roumanian songs, which are like the breath of wild mountain air, full of the voices of the birds and streams, the wailings of the wind, and the sad plaints of the human heart. There is scarce a page in the not very voluminous collection which is not marked with some untaught grace of thought or language, and which has not the charm and power of simple and strong emotion. However literal they may be, and the impression is very strongly conveyed of their absolute faithfulness, they also owe much to the fine grace and skill and to the melody of the verse into which they have been rendered in a foreign language, and the lovers of poetry owe a grateful debt to Carmen Sylva and Miss Alma Strettell, who had been already favorably known for her translations of Greek folk-songs for the artistic quality of their translations. No richer treasury of primitive poetry has been disclosed for many years.

www.ingramcontent.com/pod-product-compliance
Lightning Source LLC
Chambersburg PA
CBHW030006240426
43672CB00007B/850